GUILT AND SHAME

THE UNHOLY SIBLINGS

GUILT AND SHAME
THE UNHOLY SIBLINGS

HOW TO OVERCOME, HOW TO HEAL,
HOW TO AVOID.

BY

KURT GASSNER

Guilt And Shame The Unholy Siblings
Kurt Gassner

Impressum
My-mindguide – The publishing trademarke of trendguide Capital GmbH, Klenzestr. 42a, 80469 Munich, Germany.

Reg. Nr. HRB Munich 206639, VAT 152 123 159, CEO: Kurt Friedrich Gassner
Web: www.my-mindguide.com, mail: gassner@my-mindguide.com

Paperback ISBN: 978-3-98793-915-0
Hardback ISBN: 978-3-98793-030-0

CONTENTS

Guilt Game

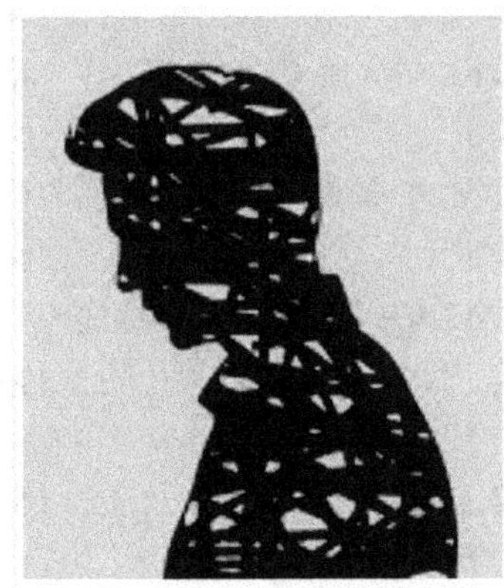 

My-mindguide.com

INTRODUCTION

WHY I Did This Book

While you may use the terms shame and guilt interchangeably to express your emotions, there is a significant distinction between them. While guilt can assist you in comprehending the impact of your actions on others, shame is an inward-directed emotion that reflects how you feel about yourself. Guilt can assist you in moving forward during recovery; however, shame keeps you stuck in the past.

Guilt and shame are necessary components of success. Allowing shame to fester can result in self-punishment and damaging actions. Shame is associated with addiction, depression, suicide, and violence, among other things, but guilt is associated with all those things in the opposite direction. While it may be tempting to punish yourself and others as you work through your shame, this is counterproductive to your recovery.

Remorse, however, might assist you in the healing process. Guilt is a sign that you're in a good recovery process since it enables you to take control of your habits and change them. In recovery, you must concentrate on guilt feelings, listen to them, and then reverse them. Once you accept responsibility for your mistakes, apologize for them, and correct them, you're well on your way to reclaiming a life that was once dominated by addiction.

Due to the distinctions between shame and guilt (who I am versus what I did). By emphasizing what someone has done wrong, guilt tends to elicit more constructive responses, especially those that seek to repair the damage. Guilt is intrinsically linked to one's opinions about right and wrong, moral and immoral behavior. When we breach one of these moral rules, we experience guilt for our acts and want to the right our wrongs (see cognitive dissonance). As a result, guilt plays a critical role in upholding individual and societal ideals of right and wrong. As such, guilt is frequently employed to resolve the disagreement.

Shame, on the other hand, accentuates what is wrong with oneself. It has a much more inward focus, and as a result, shameful parties begin to feel bad about themselves rather than their actions. As a result, behavior frequently takes an inward turn — avoiding others, concealing one's face, withdrawing from social situations. As a result, shame can present a problem, as it is frequently less constructive than guilt. Indeed, shame can result in withdrawal from social situations and subsequent defensive, aggressive, and retaliatory behavior, all of which exacerbates conflict.

Guilt and shame can both contribute significantly to the initiation and resolution of conflict. Shame, in particular, can play a significant role in the genesis of disputes. The nature of humiliation and the ensuing withdrawal and reactive lash out might escalate an already stressful situation. This can create a vicious cycle of conflict; as one party lashes out at the other, both parties' self-esteem suffers, increasing collective shame.

This results in the continuation of hostile conduct. Consider an ethnic conflict, particularly one in which members of one side have been treated as second-class citizens due to their ethnicity. As a result of their humiliation over who they are, individuals engage in retaliatory behavior and aggressive behavior. When one or both parties have been shamed for various reasons during the divorce process, the resultant responses can only exacerbate the negative parts of an already miserable experience.

Guilt and shame are both significant social influences. Both are inextricably linked to social contexts. Our concepts of guilt and shame (right and wrong) are formed in social contexts such as education, family, and employment. As a result, instructors, parents, friends, and family members must ensure that others in their immediate vicinity (especially youngsters) have a sense of self-worth. By demonstrating empathy and concern for others, we demonstrate that doing something wrong does not always reflect poorly on the individual. By separating the deed from the actor, we may assist in eliminating shame and its negative connotations while developing a healthy sense of right and wrong and, when required, guilt.

Guilt Game

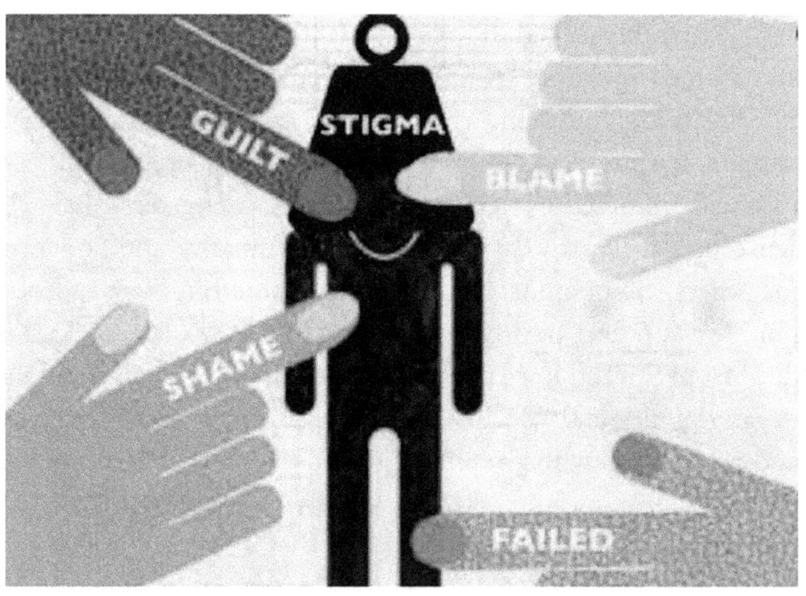

My-mindguide.com

WHAT IS GUILT?

Guilt is an unpleasant emotion that, like shame, embarrassment, and pride, has been described as a self-conscious emotion involving introspection. Individuals may experience guilt for various reasons, including acts they have performed (or believe they have committed), failure to do something they should have done, or having morally wrong thoughts.

Guilt is a natural response when one harms another. Guilt is self-centered and has a strong social component: it is believed to perform critical interpersonal functions by encouraging the repair of valuable relationships and opposing activities that could jeopardize them. However, excessive guilt may unnecessarily burden individuals who suffer from it.

What is the source of guilt, and how can it be overcome?
Most of us have experienced shame at one point or another—it's a natural part of our human nature, from guilt about not spending enough time with loved ones to refusing to say no to friends or colleagues to cheating on a partner. And, because we are all unique, we all respond differently to it.

In its purest form, guilt is a sense of regret or sadness for a past action, felt when we believe we have caused harm or violated our moral code. It serves as our moral compasses. Our ideals and how we process our emotions all influence how we respond to specific situations. Thus, where one individual may overreact to a circumstance, another may not hesitate.

Types of guilt

Guilt is classified into two types: healthy, reasonable guilt, and unhealthy, irrational guilt.

Appropriate guilt

While guilt is an unpleasant emotion, 'proper' guilt aids in regulating our social behavior. Feeling guilty for a legitimate reason indicates that our conscience and cognitive abilities function properly and prevent us from repeating or making mistakes. This provides us with the opportunity to learn from our mistakes and modify our behavior in the future.

The constant sense of guilt is called 'guilt-proneness,' and individuals who experience it are believed to have a deep connection to their own – and others' – emotions.

Irrational guilt

The illogical sort – when we incorrectly accept responsibility for a situation or overstate the suffering caused – is completely different and can be quite detrimental if we do not remedy it.

Excessive, unjustified guilt has been associated with mental diseases such as anxiety, sadness, dysphoria (perpetual unhappiness), and obsessive-compulsive disorder (OCD)2. It might lead patients to assume they are a burden to their loved ones. Guilt left unchecked can also result in decreased concentration and productivity, low mood, increased stress, and sleep deprivation. As a result, our relationships, daily activities, and overall view on life may suffer significantly.

How can we prevent these emotions from spiraling out of control?

Dr Mark Winwood, Clinical Lead for Mental Health Services at AXA Health, provides some advice for guilt.

1. Develop a mindfulness practice. Mindful meditation focuses on the breath to bring awareness to the present moment. This can help establish a connection between the mind and body and put your guilt into perspective.

2. Distract yourself with something that helps you relax — music, a book, exercise, or even a breath of fresh air.

3. Be proactive: if you believe your guilt is warranted and arrive at this conclusion rationally, take action. Make amends for your errors and move on.

4. Do not berate yourself for it. Constantly reliving past errors serves no one, least of all you.

5. Remind yourself that perfection does not exist: pursuing the ideal solution might result in mental 'gridlock,' which is counterproductive. Instead, learn to accept the 'best' choice available in the circumstances and maintain a sense of perspective.

There is no quick fix for guilty feelings. However, if warranted, it is far healthier not to eliminate them. Rather than that, accept them and utilize them to motivate you to be more optimistic in the future.

DEALING WITH GUILTY FEELINGS

Guilt is an emotional condition in which we conflict with ourselves for having done something we believe we should not have (or conversely, having not done something we believe we should have done). This can result in a persistent and difficult-to-manage emotional state.

If you are experiencing guilt, you are probably focusing on something embarrassing you did, something hurtful you did to another person or any other behavior that resulted in unpleasant consequences for you or someone else. At times, this sense of guilt can become overwhelming, and you may find yourself unable to control the severity of your sentiments.

Guilt and shame are comparable emotions in that they both involve a sense of self-loathing. Generally, guilt is related to something one has done (or not done). On the other hand, shame is frequently perceived as a sense of being an unworthy, unpleasant person. When shame becomes entrenched and ingrained in one's identity, it becomes a highly damaging and terrible feeling.

It's remarkable how quickly shame can set in for the tiniest, most insignificant events in our life. As a normal part of growing up in a social environment, most people learn to identify and deal with their feelings of guilt. Its objective is to alert us when we have done something wrong and to assist us in developing a more sophisticated understanding of our behavior and how it impacts both ourselves and others. In addition, it compels us to re-examine our behavior to avoid repeating the same error.

Unhealthy guilt

Unhealthy guilt prevents us from making mistakes; we place unreasonable expectations on ourselves and others. Guilt is unhealthy if it is excessive or causes immediate distress. Unhealthy guilt can develop as a result of the following:

- A collision of values. For instance, whereas some cultures have extremely severe regulations about sexual behavior, mainstream Australian culture is generally easygoing when it comes to sex. A child raised in Australia but with parents from another culture may shame their sexual behavior due to the clash of cultural value systems.

- Discipline that is excessively harsh or abusive. If norms of behavior are enforced in an abusive or excessively violent manner, fear of punishment can be internalized as a high degree of guilt.

- Unrealistic behavioral norms. Nobody is faultless. If you expect never to be angry, always speak the truth, and never think ill of someone, you will feel guilty a lot of the time.

- A wrongful act that has not been confessed or atoned for. Occasionally, we commit acts for which we afterwards feel guilty. If the guilt is serious enough, we may feel apprehensive about telling someone or making amends. This can result in a pernicious sense of shame and anxiety.

What harm may guilt cause?
- Make you hyper-responsible, constantly seeking to make life' right'. You may work excessively long hours, offer too

much of yourself, or be prepared to do anything to make everyone happy.

- Increase your level of conscientiousness. You may agonize over every decision you make in light of the potential negative consequences for others, even if this means ignoring your own needs and desires.

- Increase your sensitivity. You may begin to find moral dilemmas in every part of your life and develop an obsession with the precarious nature of all your actions, statements, and decisions.

- Put you in a coma. You can become so overcome by dreading doing, acting, saying, or being 'wrong' that you eventually collapse, succumb, and opt for inaction, silence, and the status quo.

- Interfere with your decision-making processes. It may become so critical to constantly be 'correct' in your selections that you are incapable of making them for fear of being incorrect.

- Conceal yourself under the mask of self-denial. You may conceal yourself beneath a façade of self-denial since it is less guilt-inducing to prioritize others. For example, you honestly feel it is preferable to serve others first, oblivious that 'guilt' might motivate such 'generous' behavior.

- Discourage you from experiencing the entire range of emotions and feelings accessible to you. When you are overcome with guilt or fear, you can become emotionally blocked, unable to appreciate the pleasant fruits of life.

- Ignore or mislead you. Because guilt is based on numerous erroneous assumptions, you may be unable to sort out your emotions. When you are suffering guilt, it is critical to remain objective with yourself so that your decisions are founded on sound, rational reasoning.

- Act as a catalyst for change. Guilt and the agony it causes can be utilized as a barometer for the need for change and a catalyst for life change.

How can we assist others in overcoming their guilt feelings, accepting them when necessary but letting them go more readily when they are not?

- **Recognize the type of guilt you are experiencing and the reason behind it.**
  Guilt is most effective in maturing and growing when our behavior has been disrespectful or hurtful to others or ourselves. For example, suppose we feel guilty for speaking an insulting word to another person or prioritizing our careers over family time by working a 60-hour week. In that case, that is a warning sign with a purpose: modify your behavior or risk harming or losing important connections. We can continue to disregard our guilt but at our peril. This is referred described as "good" or "appropriate" guilt since it aims to assist us in rerouting our behavioral compass. The issue occurs when our behavior does not require re-examination or modification. For example, many first-time mothers feel guilty about returning to work part-time, concerned that it may hurt their child's normal growth. That is just not true in most cases, and most children develop

normally and healthily even when both parents work. We feel guilty even if there is no justification for it. This is referred to as "irrational" or "unhealthy" guilt, as it serves no rational purpose.

- **Make corrections or modifications as quickly as possible.** If your guilt is justified and sensible, take action to correct the problematic behavior. Regardless of how a significant number of us are self-discipline addicts, the heaviness of our disgrace holds us back from pushing ahead. It's simple enough to apologize to someone we've insulted with an insensitive comment. However, it is more difficult to detect how your 60-hour-a-week employment may be affecting your family and adjust your work schedule (assuming that there were legitimate reasons for working 60-hours a week in the first place). Healthy guilt signals that we need to change our behavior to mend vital connections (or our self-esteem). On the other hand, unhealthy guilt exists to make us feel awful for no legitimate cause.

- **Acknowledge that you made a mistake but move forward.** If you have done something wrong or harmful, you must recognize that while you cannot undo the past, you can make amends for your behavior when and if it is appropriate. Apologize or promptly make amends for the incorrect behavior, but then let it go. The more we dwell on the belief that we need to do more, the more it will nag us and disrupt our relationships. Typically, guilt is highly situational. That is, we find ourselves in a circumstance, commit an improper or harmful act, and then feel awful for a period. Either the behavior was not as horrible as we perceived it, or time passed, and we felt less guilty. We will feel better about ourselves (and the other person) if we quickly identify and fix the problem. Obsessing over it and failing to engage in compensating behavior (such as apologizing or modifying one's negative behavior) perpetuates the unpleasant feelings. Accept and accept the inappropriacy of your behavior, then make atonement and move on.

- **Learning from our behaviors.**
The objective of guilt is not to make us feel bad for the sake of feeling awful. Instead, it attempts to draw our attention to the experience to learn something from it. When we learn from our actions, we are less likely to repeat them in the future. For example, suppose I mistakenly say anything disrespectful to another person. In that case, my shame is telling me that I should (a) apologize to the other person and (b) pause a moment before speaking. If your guilt is not motivated by an attempt to repair a genuine error in your behavior (e.g., if it is unhealthy guilt), there is not much you need to learn. Rather than focusing on stopping that behavior, you can instead focus on why a seemingly innocuous act that most people would not feel sorry about is making you feel guilty. For example, a person may feel guilty for playing a game during normal work hours. However, if they work for themselves and do not adhere to "normal work hours," they may have developed a mindset that no longer applies after years of working for others.

- **Perfection doesn't exist in anyone.**
Nobody is flawless. Pursuing perfection is doomed to failure, as perfection can never be realized. Throughout our lives, we commit errors, and a considerable lot of us decide

to go down a course that might prompt lament further down the road when we understand our slip-ups. The trick is to own your error and recognize that you are only human. Avoid days, weeks, or months of self-blame or beating your self-esteem over the fact that you should have known, acted differently, or been an ideal person. You, and others, are not. That is simply the way life is.

Guilt can be seen as an attachment to judgment and doing 'things' correctly. Rather than increasing our responsibility and accountability for our ideas, feelings, and acts, this connection decreases our responsibility and accountability since it impedes authenticity. Guilt and shame are extremely difficult to deal with, mostly because they need you to forgive yourself for whatever occurred.

Self-forgiveness necessitates openness and acceptance of oneself. By lifting the veil of guilt, we can become more connected to what we are experiencing, our thoughts and behaviors in response to that experience, and therefore more present with our experience, emotions, and ourselves.

Psychotherapy can give individuals a safe and non-judgmental space to explore their guilt and address any fears about considering behavior changes.

WHY DO WE CONSTANTLY FEEL GUILTY?

There is nothing we cannot feel guilty about: food, sex, money, work, family, friends, health, or politics.

Everything makes me feel guilty. Today, I've already felt bad for saying the wrong thing to a friend. Then I felt bad for avoiding that friend because of that. Additionally, I have not yet called my mum today: guilty. And I'm so sorry for not organizing something special for my spouses birthday. I gave my child the incorrect food: I am guilty. I've been guilty of cutting corners at work recently. I was guilty of skipping breakfast. Rather than that, I snacked: double guilt. I'm squandering all this room in a world that already lacks sufficient space: guilty, guilty.

Neither am I feeling good about my unpleasant feelings. Not with smart friends constantly reminding me of how self-absorbed, self-aggrandizing, politically conservative, and morally stunted the guilty are. I am destitute. Guilty of being guilty. I am guilty of filial guilt, fraternal guilt, male guilt, father guilt, peer guilt, work guilt, middle-class guilt, white guilt, liberal guilt, historical guilt, and Catholic guilt.

Fortunately, some people claim to be able to absolve us of guilt. But, according to Denise Duffield-Thomas, a prominent motivational speaker and author of Getting Rich, Lucky Bitch!, guilt is "one of the most common sentiments special in women experience." Guilty women, enticed by guilt into impeding their paths to increasing riches, power, status, and happiness, simply cannot seem to capitalize on their advantages. Specially woman feel that way:

"You may feel guilty for wanting more, for spending money on yourself, or for taking time away from your hectic family life to work on yourself," Duffield-Thomas adds. You may feel terrible about other people's poverty, your friend's envy, or the fact that there are hungry people in the world." Indeed, I am guilty of those acts. As such, it's reassuring to learn that I can be helped – that I can self-help. However, for that to happen, I must first recognize that a) I am worth it and b) none of these global inequality mechanisms, which are founded on historical injustices, are my responsibility.

In other words, my guilt is a manifestation not of my guilt but my innocence – even of my suffering. Only through forgiveness for wrongs for which I bear no direct responsibility can I learn to overcome my "money obstacles and enjoy a first-class life," as Duffield-Thomas puts it.

Consider this: a first-class lifestyle. This type of advice, which frames guilt as our most fundamentally restricting emotion, translates psychoanalytic and feminist concepts into commercial motivational language. The promise is that we can atone for our sins by earning money.

This concept may resonate particularly well in the German language, where guilt and debt are synonymous with Schuld. Consider Max Weber's concept on how the "spirit of capitalism" conflates our material and spiritual wealth because what you earn also serves as a barometer of your spiritual virtue, as it is contingent on your aptitude for hard effort, discipline, and self-denial.

However, what Weber refers to as "salvation anxiety" inside the Protestant work ethic has the opposite impact of the self-help manual's promise to cleanse entrepreneurs of guilt. Indeed, according to Weber, the capitalist quest of profit does not absolve one of guilt but actively exacerbates it — for there can be no rest for the wicked in an economy that preaches stagnation.

Thus, the shame that obstructs and hinders us simultaneously motivates us to work and become obsessively productive to absolve ourselves of guilt by our good acts. It's a contradiction that may explain why some go to such extremes to avoid feeling guilty, either by blaming others or themselves or by sacrificing their wellbeing for the sake of avoiding the dreadful emotion.

How powerful is guilt? With its inflationary logic, guilt appears to have accumulated over time, if anything. Even though we will more often than not fault religion for sentencing a man to live as a heathen, the responsibility that might have been related with explicit indecencies - indecencies for which strict networks could recommend fitting repentance - presently seems to surface regarding pretty much anything: food, sex, cash, work, joblessness, recreation, wellbeing, wellness, legislative issues, family, companions, partners, outsiders, diversion, travel, and the climate, to give some examples.

Equally, anyone who believes that public humiliation rites are a horrific relic of the medieval past hasn't been paying much attention to our online lives. However, you can't expect to remain anonymous on social media for very long until someone starts pointing fingers at you for something you did. Yet it's difficult to believe that our age's reigning spirit, the jealous and resentful troll, would have such easy pickings if he didn't already detect a smell of guilt-susceptibility wafting from his prey.

This was not intended. The modern era's great crusaders were intended to remove our guilt. Guilt has been the target of numerous high-minded critiques, with modern intellectuals accusing it of sucking the life out of us and contributing to our psychological degeneration. It was asserted that it renders us feeble (Nietzsche), neurotic (Freud), and inauthentic (Freud) (Sartre).

Several critical views gained academic legitimacy throughout the twentieth century, most notably in the humanities. These were theories that attempted to demonstrate – whether through class, racism, or gender relations – how we are all cogs in a greater system of power. We may contribute to oppressive regimes, but we are also at the mercy of forces greater than ourselves.

However, this raises concerns regarding personal responsibility: since our unique circumstance is supported by a complex web of social and economic interactions, how can any individual truly claim to be in complete control of or responsible for their own life? When seen in this detached manner, shame can appear an unproductive relic from a less self-aware era.

When used imprecisely, explanatory theories can provide believers with a failsafe system for determining precisely which position to hold, with impunity, regarding almost everything - as if one could take out an insurance policy guaranteeing one will always be correct. Often, too, that is the extent to which such critique leads – into a right-thinking that does not always translate into right-acting.

To a religious person, the thought that our intellectual frameworks may be as much a reaction to our guilt as they are a solution may seem familiar. After all, in the biblical tale, Adam "falls" when tempted by the fruit of the tree of knowledge. " knowing " leads him out of the Garden of Eden and into an ongoing exile. His guilt serves as a persistent, nagging reminder that he has made a mistake.

Nonetheless, even within that source, we see how man's guilt can be deceiving – as cunning and alluring as the serpent that led him wrong. For if a man has sinned by tasting knowledge, the guilt that punishes him repeats his offence: with all its finger-wagging and tone of "I told you so," guilt comes across as frighteningly knowing. It holds us captive, as psychologist Adam Phillips (Adam Phillips contributes often to the London Review of Books. He has been dubbed "the Martin Amis of British psychoanalysis" by The Times for his "brilliantly hilarious and frequently genuinely frightening" work, and John Banville has characterized him as "one of the finest literary stylists in the language, a modern Emerson." His approach to the new Freud edition is congruent with his own views on psychoanalysis, which he regards as a type of persuasive rhetoric. Put it to that tedious and repetitive voice within our heads that constantly corrects, criticizes, censors, judges, and finds fault with us but "never delivers us any news about ourselves." Yet, we appear to have already a sense of who we are and what we are capable of in our guilt feelings.

Could this perhaps be the source of our guilt? Not our ignorance – but rather our presumption of ignorance? Our frantic need to be certain of ourselves, even when we believe we are worthless, useless, and the pits? When we feel guilty, we have the consolation of certainty — of finally knowing the proper way to feel, which is horrible.

This may explain why we are drawn to crime dramas: they satisfy our want for certainty, regardless of how bleak that certainty is. At the start of a detective story, we know a crime but have no idea who committed it. Case closed: We know who the guilty party is by the end of the story. To put it briefly, shame transforms our ignorance into knowledge in popular language.

However, for a psychoanalyst, sentiments of guilt do not always correlate with being guilty in the eyes of the law. While our sentiments of guilt may be a confession, they typically occur before the charge of any crime, the details of which are unknown even to the guilty party.

Thus, while the stories we favor may reveal guilt, it is also possible that our guilt serves as a cover.

Although "the fall" is a biblical account, set aside your religious beliefs for a time. One may equally well narrate a more contemporary and secular account of man's fall. It is a "narrative" with innumerable narrators, maybe none finer or more passionate than Theodor Adorno, the German Jewish postwar critic. In the aftermath of the Holocaust, Adorno famously claimed that everybody who survives in a world capable of producing Auschwitz is guilty, at least to the extent that they remain a member of the same civilization.

In other words, guilt is an indisputable historical fact. It is our modern people's pact. As such, Adorno asserts that we all share a common responsibility to be vigilant following Auschwitz, lest we relapse into the modes of thinking, believing, and behaving that precipitated this guilty judgment. Making sense after Auschwitz entails accepting responsibility for its cruelty.

Thus, for Adorno, knowledge imprisons us rather than protects us. This may appear surprising to a modern mentality. That said, arguably the most unexpected aspect of Adorno's portrayal of guilt is the notion reflected in his query "whether one may continue living after Auschwitz – particularly if one who survived by accident, one who should have been killed, may continue living." His sheer survival necessitates coldness, the fundamental basis of bourgeois subjectivity, without which there would have been no Auschwitz; this is the heinous sin of the spared".

According to Adorno, the guilt of Auschwitz is shared by all western civilization. Still, it is the guilt he imagined would be felt most acutely by "one who escaped by accident, one who should have been slaughtered" - the second world war Jewish survivor.

Adorno, who had arrived in New York from Europe in early 1938, was almost certainly attesting to his own guilt. Yet his insight is consistent with that of psychologists who worked with concentration camp survivors following the war; they discovered that "guilty feelings accompanied by shame, self-condemnatory tendencies, and self-accusations are experienced by victims of persecution and appear to be experienced much less (if at all) by perpetrators of persecution."

What does it mean when victims feel terrible, but perpetrators are not held accountable? Are objective guilt (having committed a crime) and subjective guilt (feeling guilty) mutually exclusive?

After the war, "survival guilt" was frequently interpreted due to the victim's association with the aggressor. The survivor may later struggle to forgive themselves since others died in their place - why am I still alive when others perished? – Additionally, she may feel guilty for what she was compelled to collude with to survive. This does not have to suggest any wrongdoing on her side; her shame may simply be an unconscious method of expressing her prior preference for others to suffer instead of her.

On this logic, it may be reasonable to view survivor's guilt as a subset of the guilt we all carry when conscious or unconscious. We rejoice when others suffer rather than ourselves. It's not a pleasant feeling, but it's not difficult to understand either. Even so, there is something profoundly unsettling in accepting that survivors of the most heinous atrocities should have any responsibility for their survival. Rather than that, shouldn't we attempt to rescue the survivor from her (in our opinion) erroneous emotions of guilt and establish her perfect innocence without a blemish or quibble?

According to intellectual historian Ruth Leys, this natural urge resulted in the emergence of the concept of "the survivor" following World War II, along with a shift in emphasis away from the victim's emotions of guilt and toward an insistence on the victim's innocence. Leys contends that this transition occurred due to the concept of guilt being replaced by its close cousin, shame.

The distinction is critical. The victim who feels guilt has an inner existence, with aims and desires – whereas the victim who feels shame appears to have received it externally. As a result, trauma sufferers appear to be objects rather than history subjects.

Thus, shame informs us about who we are, not what we do – or would like to do. Thus, this well-intentioned shift in emphasis may have had the effect of depriving the survivor of the agency.

It's tempting to believe that survival guilt is an outlier occurrence, considering the victims' total impotence in the aftermath of such experiences. However, as we will see, attempting to deny the reality of another's guilt frequently results in denying their intentions as well. Consider the issue of "liberal guilt," the kind of guilt that we all despise.

Liberal guilt has become a catch-all term for those acutely aware of a lack of social, political, and economic fairness yet do not bear its weight. According to cultural analyst Julie Ellison, it first gained traction in the United States in the 1990s due to the left's post-1945 fragmentation and a loss of faith in the utopian politics of collective action that had defined an earlier generation of radicals. The guilty liberal has abandoned the collective and recognizes that she acts in her self-interest. Thus, her guilt reflects the chasm between her compassion for the other's suffering and her willingness to act actively to alleviate it - which, as it turns out, is not much.

As such, her guilt incites considerable hostility in others, not least in the individual who perceives himself to be the liberal's victim. This individual, dubbed "the victim," is well aware of how rarely the empathy he inspires in the guilty liberal will result in meaningful structural or political changes for him.

Rather than that, the only "power" that can be channeled in his direction is the moral or affective power to make people who are wealthier than he feels even more terrible about the privileges they are unwilling to give up.

However, how in command of her emotions is the guilty liberal? Ellison believes such is not the case. Due to the difficulty of confuting feelings, her guilt frequently attacks her unexpectedly, rendering her excessively theatrical, exhibitionist, and even hysterical. She senses a "loss of control" in her guilt, even though she is always aware of an audience in front of whom she believes she must demonstrate how spectacularly sorry she is. Thus, her guilt is a form of "acting out," signaling an unease in the liberal who does not know herself as well as her guilt would have her believe.

The concept of guilt as an inhibitory emotion corroborates a frequently levelled criticism of liberal guilt: that, for all the misery it causes, it fails to propel the guilty subject to effect real political change.

However, what if the liberal's guilt serves another purpose: to provide relief from something she may (unconsciously) feel even worse about: the absence of a solid identity that defines who she is, what her responsibilities are, and where they end?

If one characteristic can characterize the notoriously fuzzy liberal, it is probably guilt. Liberal guilt alludes to a certain socioeconomic (middle class), racial (white), and geopolitical (developed world) context. As such, despite the agony it causes those who suffer from it, it may be soothing for someone whose true neurosis is the sense that her identity is so fluid and moving that she can never be certain where she stands.

If this is her primary worry, one could imagine her guilt as an emotion that informs her of her by telling her who she is failing to be for others. Who or what is a liberal? She who suffers for the sake of those who suffer more. (I am aware of what I am speaking.)

This may help to understand why liberal values have been under increasing attack in recent years. To her detractors, the liberal is truly guilty. She is guilty of:

1. Secretly resenting victims for the way their suffering affects her.
2. Deflecting attention away from them and toward herself.
3. Having the arrogance to exhibit her self-lacerations.
4. Doing virtually nothing to disrupt the status quo.

In other words, feeling guilty is part of the problem, not the solution. And yet, this criticism is also a target of the same charge. Given that criticizing someone for feeling guilty simply serves to increase their guilt, guilt has proven to be a difficult adversary - one that its numerous modern adversaries have yet to overcome.

Thus, once again, in the instance of liberal guilt, we meet emotion so devilishly fluid that it replicates the problem while confessing it. Because, of course, there is a type of guilt that does not motivate us to act but rather inhibits us from acting. This type of guilt transforms the ambiguity of our interpersonal relationships (and our responsibility for others) into an object of certainty and knowledge.

However, because the "object" in this case is our own self, we can see how liberal guilt, like conservative guilt, transforms guilt into a form of shame. Indeed, shame may be a more apt description of what motivates the guilty liberal's public and private self-condemnation.

However, before we label liberals "guilty as charged" – as in guilty of the wrong kind of guilt – it's important to recall that many have interpreted survival guilt in the same way. For, as we noted in that example, by attempting to "rescue" the victim from her guilt, the victim loses the exact thing that can distinguish her from the objectifying aggression that has attacked her: a feeling of her own goals and desires, however aggressive, perverse, or thwarted they may be.

Thus, it is essential to preserve the concept of survivor's guilt (and, despite obvious differences, liberal guilt) in order to restore the survivor (or liberal) the agency necessary if she is to have a future that will not be bound to repeat the past ad infinitum by clearing or resolving her guilt.

If religion is frequently blamed for presenting man as a sinner, the secular effort to absolve man of his guilt has largely failed. According to Italian philosopher Giorgio Agamben, subjective innocence is a relic of a bygone era, the age of the tragic hero. For instance, Oedipus is someone whose objective of his subjective innocence matches guilt (murder, incest) as a man who acts before he knows. As opposed to Oedipus, who killed with his own hands, Agamben argues that today's man is objectively blameless but personally culpable (he knows that his comforts and securities have been paid for by someone, somewhere, probably in blood).

By falsely promising a blank slate contingent on man's historical and intellectual emancipation, modernity may have not only failed to eradicate man's subjective guilt but may have worsened it. For many, a modern man is guilty of less than his acts but more of an addiction to a version of knowledge that appears to have harmed his capacity for action. As such, the theological designation of man as a sinner - a fallen, abject, perpetually compromised, but the active, effective, and adaptable creature – begins to appear more comfortable.

This perspective also has a lot in common with a particular psychoanalytic interpretation of guilt as a repressed form of aggressiveness or rage directed toward those we need and love (God, parents, guardians, whoever we depend on for our own survival). However, even if guilt often blocks all other (buried, repressed, unconscious) emotions, this is not a justification to avoid feeling it. After all, feelings are what you must be prepared to feel if they are to move you or if they are to elicit another emotion.

GUILTY FEELINGS: WHAT IS A GUILT COMPLEX? AND FIVE INDICATES THAT YOU POSSESS ONE

Numerous diverse factors might contribute to guilt. Each experience of guilt is unique. For example, there are times when one feels guilty for not sharing the same sentiments as a friend or colleague. Guilt is a more subjective emotion. As a result, your moral code plays a critical part in establishing a sensation of guilt.

Although the environment plays a role, the way a person was raised and the people with whom they associates affect the types of guilt that individual experiences. All these factors contribute to the formation of a guilty complex. According to psychologists, five distinct circumstances result in guilt.

Continue reading to learn more about the five distinct types of guilt complexes, some typical indicators that may indicate you have one, what to do about it, and frequently asked questions regarding guilt.

How Is a Guilt Complex Defined?

According to the Cambridge English dictionary, guilt is defined as "a sense of anxiety or dissatisfaction that you experience as a result of having committed a wrong, such as harming another person." In this scenario, the injustice could be genuine or imagined. When you do something incorrectly or believe you have done something incorrectly, you feel awful about it and may attempt to rectify the situation. That is the nature of guilt.

However, a guilt complex is a powerful sense of guilt that is frequently present regardless of whether you are accountable for the wrongs or shortcomings. Despite the individual's attempts, the individual's guilt for routine behaviors is intense and challenging to manage. Often, it causes misery for them and those around them, as it creates self-doubt, humiliation, and worry, and may even sway the person toward drug abuse to cope with their guilt and shame. It also may bring up past mistakes and manifest as unresolved guilt, further complicating your ability to cope with daily activities.

Understanding guilt and guilt complexes are the first steps toward resolving your or a loved one's problem with guilt and shame. There are five basic guilt complexes that we will explore in-depth, along with advice on how to overcome them: a bad deed, guilt thoughts, fake guilt, compassion guilt, and successor/guilt. survivor's

What Are Guilt Complex Theories?

Theory 1

According to some conventional psychologists, guilt is acquired and founded in our childhood conduct. It is associated with anxiety and develops during the formative years of life. According to some psychologists, children learn guilt at a young age. If they have a wrong attitude toward guilt or experience excessive guilt as a youngster, guilt may develop into one of their most substantial feelings.

Theory 2
On the other hand, contemporary psychologists believe that guilt complexes have their origins in cognitive activities. Guilt is a complex emotion that occurs when someone commits an error or believes they have committed one.

Numerous complex guilt examples include individuals suffering guilt under the completely erroneous belief that they did anything wrong or caused harm. These negative feelings are frequently associated with the individual's misperception, overthinking, or overgeneralization of outcomes, as well as their failure to reason their views coherently. When someone feels guilty, they frequently experience bodily symptoms such as:

- Headaches
- Worry
- Muscle pain
- Nausea
- Tearfulness
- Insomnia
- Fatigue

Understanding guilt is not limited to its theories and symptoms; we would also examine the five distinct situations that result in guilt and advice for dealing with a guilt complex and how to cope with each situation and seek outside assistance.

Guilty Signs: Five Situations That Produce Guilt

1. An Incorrect Action

A person is more likely to feel guilty when they have done something wrong, such as harming another person's physical or emotional health. In this case, they feel guilty when the repercussions of their wrongful conduct become apparent or when the individual crosses their bounds. Additionally, it can arise when someone violates their morality by lying, cheating, or stealing. Occasionally, a person may feel guilty for breaking a promise made to themself. For instance, you may commit yourself to abstain from drinking, taking drugs, smoking, or overeating. When we break our obligations to ourselves and others, we are unavoidably filled with guilt since we are aware that we have done wrong.

Overcoming Guilt for Wrongful Actions Tip No. 1.

It is reasonable to feel guilty in situations where you have harmed yourself or others. If you felt no shame in these scenarios, it could signify a more serious and complex psychological disorder such as Narcissistic Personality Disorder or Antisocial Personality Disorder. Recognizing that whatever has happened has happened and that you have no control over it is crucial for overcoming your feelings of guilt. Accepting guilt, apologizing, and then attempting to avoid it from happening again is the best approach to deal with it. This would prevent it from developing into chronic guilt.

If your guilt stems from transgressing your limits, morals, or ethics—such as excessive alcohol or drug usage, lying, or cheating—the simplest method to prevent these troubles from recurring is to break these behaviors. This can be achieved by looking for a proficient help from an instructor or restoration program or by enrolling the help of a companion or relative. Rather than constantly feeling guilty, which would accomplish nothing but make you sad.

2. Guilty Thoughts

This type of guilt is extremely normal, as many of us occasionally have negative thoughts. However, they might occasionally result in guilt. The individual frequently feels terrible for having these negative ideas yet does not act on them. Even contemplating doing anything that violates one's ethical code, such as being dishonest, unfaithful, or criminal, can induce feelings of guilt and shame in the individual. For instance, if you lusted after someone other than your significant other, partner, spouse, or loved one or considered physically injuring another person, these thoughts will certainly result in guilt. According to many psychologists, this is a tough guilt complex because you did not act on your thoughts; there was no actual action.

Overcoming Guilty Thoughts Tip 2.

If you feel guilty about having immoral or improper thoughts, it is preferable to address them and your feelings about them. If you can't control your ideas, you can design a plan to alter them so that you don't submit to them and carry out the deeds.

Most people will attempt to dismiss, repress, or "shove under the rug" these thoughts. This is not. However, the best approach to cope with them. These thoughts may eventually prompt you to take action. Accept that you've thought these thoughts and make a conscious effort to reduce their strength and influence on you. Begin by selecting a more optimistic concept to replace the negative one. Additionally, you can try other hobbies such as dancing, jogging, or yoga to help clear your thoughts.

3. "False" Guilt

Emotional complexities can be extremely complicated. Most people are unhappy due to their own unreasonable and inaccurate beliefs about themselves, others, and even the world. Occasionally, we experience guilt even when we believe we have done nothing wrong. In these instances, we may feel just as bad as when we commit an error. For instance, like a guilty pleasure, we can fantasize about a competitive coworker losing their job or secretly wishing for the demise of a friend's or ex's relationship. These thoughts are frequently the result of our spiteful impulses, but we know deep down that they are unreasonable somehow. However, refuting these beliefs and thoughts remains tough.

In extreme circumstances, individuals have committed no wrongdoing but convince themselves that they have. You may be amazed to discover that this isn't simply an issue for individuals. As a result, the individual prefers to shun self-beneficial activities, believing they are not deserving. It frequently develops into persistent guilt, impeding the individual's chances of achievement.

How to Get Rid of "False" Guilt Tip 3.

Guilt can be overwhelming, so before you beat yourself up for doing something wrong, ask yourself whether you actually did something wrong or just believe you did. Distorting your memory of events only reinforces the perception that you were at fault. If you can think about the occurrence and ask yourself questions, you can then analyze and assess whether there is genuinely anything to feel guilty about. If coping gets increasingly difficult, you might seek professional assistance.

4. Compassion Guilt

There are times when individuals feel as though they cannot provide adequate assistance to another. Think about a friend or relative who has recently gone through a divorce or passed away. It's time to return to your other responsibilities, such as your job or even caring for your own family, after spending so much time with your friend or family. Consequently, you begin to feel guilty because you cannot meet the standards you have set for yourself to support them. Compassion fatigue is the term psychologists use to describe these events that result in guilt. These circumstances may result in burnout for two reasons:

1) You attempt to care for another person while simultaneously attending to your own needs and duties.
2) The overpowering sense of guilt combined with the exhaustion associated with caring for others might deplete you.

Getting Over Compassion Guilt Tip 3.

You must remember that you can choose to help someone and make sacrifices to support your friend or family member. However, you must recognize that you also must look out for yourself. Suffering from guilt will only exacerbate your emotional state, preventing you from being effective assistance and ultimately leading to burnout. To be there for someone else, you must first be there for yourself. Remind yourself of this whenever you become aware of your compassion guilt.

5. Successor/Survivor Guilt

Have you ever felt bad about performing well when another individual struggled? This circumstance may induce guilt. Psychologists refer to these scenarios as survivor guilt. A classic example is when a friend or family member has lost another loved one or has been affected by a calamity; occasionally, individuals feel guilty since they are better than the mourning person.

Survivor guilt can also affect those who have achieved greater success than their family or friends. For instance, college students who gain a higher degree frequently feel guilty about their achievement compared to family members who did not attend college. They aspire to excel but frequently feel guilty for being afforded more advanced possibilities than their families or friends.

Get Over Successor/Survivor Guilt Tip 5.

The people who love you will be happy for you, so tell yourself that. Remember that failing on purpose will not heal someone of their condition or bring them back, nor will it change how people feel about you. Consider the knowledge and accomplishments you've achieved as a homage to your family and your roots. If you've accomplished anything significant, take pride in your accomplishments. You worked hard for them. Don't allow anyone to make you feel bad about being your best self.

What is Guilt Complex Therapy, and Are There Alternative Treatments Options?

Along with attempting the "Getting Over Guilt" strategies outlined above, cognitive therapy and psychotherapy may also be beneficial. This treatment teaches individuals how to break free from the thinking processes that generate guilt—regardless of whether an act was committed. In addition, individuals who are perpetually tormented by guilt are also taught to develop a greater awareness of their attitudes and sentiments, including recognizing when they have done something wrong and avoiding overthinking, overgeneralizing, or overcomplicating situations.

Bear in mind that if you can alter your thoughts, you also can also alter your emotions. For example, once you recognize that you have an erroneous perception of yourself as a cause of other people's suffering, you can alter your attitudes and ideas to avoid experiencing guilty feelings.

WHY DO I FEEL GUILTY WHEN THERE IS NO EVIDENCE TO SUPPORT IT?

No one is born feeling guilty.

Do you have a nagging sense that you've always done something wrong but can't put your finger on what it is? Or perhaps you're the first to take the blame when anything goes wrong...

Whatever you accomplish or how hard you work to assist others, you can't shake the feeling that you're never quite "enough." You feel inferior, insufficient in some way - but you're not sure why.

If you frequently feel guilty, you may identify with some of the following thoughts:

- "I am a selfish person if I do not put others first."
- "It is my obligation to ensure that everyone is happy."
- "I am not as "excellent" as other folks."
- "Always put the needs of others ahead of my own."

Why am I so guilty for no apparent reason?

First, let us state unequivocally that no one is born thinking of feeling this way. If you're feeling bad for no apparent reason, the source of your guilt is almost always traceable to your history.

Each has an "inner critic," but some are considerably louder. Your inner critic sounds like (and the stories it tells) is highly influenced by the messages you received as a child.

Consider a few scenarios in which this could occur.

Someone who grew up in a success-oriented environment is likely to have a highly pressurizing inner critic telling them to work harder "or else."

Similarly, someone who grew up in a cruel or negligent household is more likely to have one that is more severe, telling them they are "worthless" or will "never make it."

At first, the inner critic emerges as a protective mechanism. As children, we are defenseless - we rely on adults for protection and care to exist. Our inner critic provides an important function. It is formed to assist us in remaining "in check," behaving in a way that fits in, and avoiding more scorn or disgrace. As such, it aids in our survival by ensuring that we keep the connection we so urgently require.

The issue is that, over time, these "voices" become ingrained in our personalities. They morph into us. And while they may have aided us in our youth, they prevent us from realizing our full potential as adults.

If guilt is a common sensation for you, these beliefs about yourself and what you should do were almost certainly passed down to you. This may have been stated directly (in straightforward, unambiguous terms) or indirectly (implied through actions).

Frequently, those who were excessively reliant on children — either physically or emotionally – develop a guilt-tripping inner conversation. Consider the responsibility of caring for a chronically ill or depressed parent. Here, the child felt obligated to protect and care for their parent.

Perhaps there was a sensation that no matter what you did, it was never enough. Alternatively, the guilt may have been induced by subliminal messages ("I don't know what I'd do without you," "Don't worry about me, I'll be fine").

Whatever it was, you were taught that it was your obligation to look after others. As a result, you discover your worth through pleasing and serving others.

The issue is that you cannot please everyone, and in attempting to do so, you risk losing sight of your own needs. Indeed, you may hesitate to acknowledge what you have wanted.

As a result, you may experience shame whenever you need to express yourself or maintain limits. Deep down, you believe that if you direct your attention to your own needs, you will suffer the rejection you feared as a child.

Notifications to be on the lookout for
- You are a people pleaser
- You feel bad when you disagree with others
- You have difficulties identifying what you want in life (both large and small decisions)
- You have a penchant for putting other people's needs ahead of your own
- You can "feel" other people's emotions
- You are unable to bear hurting other people's feelings
- You feel guilty for requesting what you desire.
- You struggle with self-advocacy.
- You frequently take on the role of "caretaker," whether with friends or relationships.
- You have difficulty negotiating and find it difficult to request raises at work.
- You have difficulty delegating because you are uncomfortable asking for assistance.

How to stop constantly feeling guilty

Guilt serves a purpose — it illuminates our errors. However, it loses that meaning when it remains with us for no apparent reason.

Living with the persistent sense that we've done something wrong is not only taxing, but it can also create significant anxiety and long-term damage.

Rather than diverting your energy to meet the demands of others, you must learn to prioritize your own.

This self-blame-inducing voice can be helped to be identified and eliminated through therapy. To destabilize and undermine it, a variety of methods might be used, including sabotage and denial.

The first step toward overcoming guilt is recognizing that it is not your responsibility to bear it. Recognize why it exists and practice self-compassion. You may even choose to express gratitude for the lessons you've learned along the way. You're probably the type of naturally empathic person, which is an admirable trait. This empathy just needs to be directed in the appropriate direction – and, crucially, never at the expense of one's wellbeing.

GUILT AND HYPERTENSION

You received your lab results from your clinic and discovered that you are not as healthy as you believed. Your blood pressure has not decreased, and your cholesterol level has remained elevated. Perhaps you've already tried some of the "go-to" tips — cut back on salt, walk 10,000 steps each day, quit smoking — but nothing stays for long. Perhaps your spouse labels the refrigerator door with "healthy reminders" – still no effect. Thus, you inquire as to what you are doing incorrectly. What could you have accomplished more effectively in the past? As health magazines recommend, should you eat salmon and quinoa twice a week? Should you give up the gaming system that has anchored your buttocks to the couch? You ask yourself all these things, but they just serve to increase your guilt over your current condition of health. And the guilt is a drag.

Is it your responsibility that you are at risk of developing heart disease?

As with many other unpleasant feelings, guilt can benefit our wellbeing. It's a method of admitting that we have fallen short. As a brief feeling, it can be adaptive and generate beneficial change. However, constant guilt – chronic guilt – is counterproductive and can result in chronic stress. Anything that puts your body under prolonged stress will raise your blood pressure. In other words, if you have heart health concerns — high blood pressure, high cholesterol, or diabetes – those problems are exacerbated when you are continually guilty about them.

Persistent guilt can result in chronic stress, which might result in hypertension.

Given the stresses of contemporary society, modern advertising, and familial inheritance, I would argue that it is truly not your fault if you are at risk of developing heart disease. External variables are frequently impossible to control. The only flaw is allowing your guilt to spiral out of control and failing to utilize the tools that make it simple to regain control of your health. Thus, how do you alleviate guilt? We give some thoughts and suggestions to assist you and assist you in assisting yourself.

Guilt has a psychological and bodily impact on us.
To begin, recognize that guilt pervades our mental space. Guilt erodes our self-esteem and inhibits us from pursuing our goals. Chronic guilt can result in anxiety, and anxiety can result in various stress-related health problems over time. In addition, your bad emotions permeate the human body's physiological function, and sometimes physical ailments arise in response to these negative emotions. These can include ulcers and headaches and a variety of other physical symptoms that may appear unrelated.

Notably, it has been demonstrated that guilt increases cortisol levels. Cortisol is a stress hormone that activates the "fight or flight" response in your body. While cortisol is beneficial for defending against a potential threat, chronic exposure can raise blood pressure and increase your risk of heart disease, diabetes, decreased immunity, and other long-term diseases. Regardless of how guilt manifests in your physical health, chronic symptoms associated with unpleasant emotions can negatively impact the long-term trajectory of your health.

Blood pressure is an excellent predictor of your degree of stress.

When we are stressed, our blood pressure changes. As previously stated, numerous stress hormones such as cortisol can cause an increase in blood pressure. This occurs almost soon following the occurrence of stress. Stress hormones cause blood pressure to rise over normal levels, which is bad for both the mind and the body when they are regularly released. Preexisting hypertension is worsened by this. It's a never-ending cycle that you must break free of!

The first step toward wellness is to end the internal guilt trip.

Even if you've been practicing self-care for some time or are just learning about it for the first time, remember to take care of yourself.

This is unique to each individual. Some people benefit from yoga or exercise, while others would rather receive a massage or travel to scenic locations to watch the sunset. Do whatever it is that makes you happier and more positive. Make sure to maintain your self-confidence and drive to regain the reins of power.

Eliminating guilt alleviates tension, boosts confidence, and lowers blood pressure.

Recognize that you are not alone in this journey. Indeed, your health care app is available directly on your phone (or your Apple Watch). Because monitoring your blood pressure is one of the simplest ways to monitor your health, the Hello Heart team created a multifunctional and simple-to-use app for monitoring your blood pressure (iOS, Android). We wish to assist you in initiating the healing process and hope you will take full advantage of our assistance. Hello, Heart is a free personal health care application that can assist you in regaining your equilibrium at your speed. Take each step cautiously. Today, download the Hello Heart app (iOS, Android) and rediscover your true potential! Only a lack of utilization of available resources will be viewed as an error on your part, not your current situation.

THE SCIENCE OF SHAME

Shame is a strong emotion that can significantly affect your life.

While systemic racism is not new, many white people are only now confronting their role in white supremacy, resulting in some complex emotions. While a healthy dosage of remorse for our collective participation in anti-Black racism might encourage individuals to listen, learn, and improve, experts, warn that wallowing in shame may have the opposite effect.

While both guilt and shame arise from a sense of wrongdoing, understanding the difference can impact your ability to abstain from harmful habits. According to Jena Field, a psychologist based in London, guilt is focused on a specific behavior — which is why psychologists refer to guilt as a "moral and adaptive emotion" —. In contrast, shame is focused on the wrongdoer's identity.

As a result of this anxiety response, we tend to get defensive or hide, which makes it difficult to step back and consider what we might have done differently.

According to Lea Flego, a marital and family therapist in Oregon, shame may prevent individuals from changing their behaviors, which can be detrimental in the fight against systematic racism. "If we as allies feel shame, we will be unable to accept the times we have benefited from a racist culture," she explains. "Criticism hurts so much, and as humans, we naturally seek to avoid that kind of pain."

While guilt can be beneficial, shame is detrimental.
The danger response that many people experience during shame is significant for its ineffectiveness. According to Gerald Fishkin, a psychologist based in California and author of The Science of Shame, shame is related to the limbic system. That is the brain region that affects the autonomic nervous system, which is responsible for the fight-or-flight response.

According to Fishkin, guilt relates to activity in the prefrontal cortex, the brain's logical-thinking region. Therefore, guilt can also stimulate limbic system activity. (This is why it can seem so anxious.) However, because the stress response is related to prefrontal function, the adrenaline rush aids in your progress toward repairing whatever went wrong.

"Guilt is a cognitive response to a violation of a learned value, requiring thought and action," Fishkin explains.

"Acute shame experiences, dubbed "shame attacks" by some therapists, can result in abrupt physical changes associated with a panic response."

On the other hand, shame is more primal and does not often require cognitive processes such as logic or reasoning. Instead, it is a natural stress response that "takes over" the brain. According to research, when the limbic stress response in the brain is activated, the prefrontal cortex, which regulates rational reasoning, becomes less functioning.

Additionally, scientific study has established a relationship between guilt and the physiological desire for self-preservation: Shame activates the same brain circuits that cause people to flee physical danger. "Shame has no relation to cognition at all. When shame is activated, we become emotionally hijacked, with no prefrontal activity," Fishkin explains. "We are wired to desire anonymity and invisibility."

That form of stress, the natural impulse to conceal oneself, has the potential to cause both immediate and long-term bodily alterations. For example, acute shame experiences, referred to by some therapists as a "shame attack," can result in immediate physical changes connected with the terror response. Field notes that shame frequently manifests as a "sunken" body posture, a physical manifestation of a desire to vanish. Additionally, because it is a stress reaction, it might trigger classic sympathetic activation signs such as flushed cheeks, raised body temperature, sweat, or nausea.

'Toxic shame' can have long-lasting bodily and psychological consequences.

Often, shame results from trauma. For instance, Fishkin asserts that newborns who have endured trauma or children who have never developed stable relationships with their parents frequently have what he refers to as "toxic shame" later in life — a type of deep-seated sense of unlovability and unworthiness.

While most people experience brief moments of guilt, those who suffer toxic shame feel it in every aspect of their identity. "[Toxic] shame exacerbates our worst worries," Fishburn argues. "It is the dread of not being good enough, of being unimportant, of being a failure."

This form of guilt can have long-lasting bodily and psychological consequences. For example, the persistent "I'm broken" or "I'm bad" messages in the brain can generate feelings of hopelessness or powerlessness, which can look a lot like depression, according to Arielle Schwartz, a clinical psychologist in Colorado.

This sort of shame has been linked to increased sadness, anxiety, and eating disorders in scientific studies. However, many believe that in most of her clinical clients, she discovers shame lurking beneath anger, despair, and anxiety: "By peeling away all the layers, you will reach the heart of humiliation."

"With shame, I'm afraid to go within and own my flaws because doing so would imply that I'm awful or not good enough."

Toxic shame, according to Fishkin, can also raise the likelihood of substance abuse and addiction, owing to its inherent isolating nature. Individuals who believe they are worthless may abuse alcohol or drugs owing to their lack of exposure to the pleasant, fuzzy feelings associated with oxytocin, the social bonding hormone.

"Especially at times of major stress, such as the epidemic and social and political strain that are occurring right now,"

Flego says, "this is a time when we should be attempting to connect." "However, shame makes us gaze down and prevents us from interacting with others."

Unlike guilt, which typically motivates people to change, shame can sometimes obstruct personal growth, causing people to feel "stuck." That is the dichotomy of shame: you feel bad about yourself and want to feel better. However, the self-reflection necessary to enhance your life is probably a frightening concept. As a result, you maintain a state of fight or flight to defend yourself, and the cycle continues.

"With shame, I'm afraid to go within and own my flaws because doing so would imply that I'm awful or not good enough," Flego explains. "And if we are unable to see ourselves clearly, we will be unable to improve."

Treating shame

For many mental illnesses, such as anxiety and depression, cognitive behavioral therapy is the gold standard of treatment, as it focuses on questioning thoughts that may result in harmful behaviors. However, shame is a physiological reaction to a threat rather than a cognitive process, and it often demands a different strategy.

Fishkin employs compassion-focused therapy, which teaches individuals to view themselves and others more compassionately. In a 2016 study, most participants with trauma-related shame reported experiencing significant reductions in both shame and trauma symptoms.

Schwartz believes that self-compassion is perhaps the most critical puzzle component for everyone who faces shame in any capacity. Self-compassion, as defined by psychologist Kristen

Neff, creator of the widely used "self-compassion scale," is being kind and understanding toward oneself at times of suffering and failure and recognizing one's circumstances as part of the larger human experience. And her research indicates that it assists individuals in overcoming fear and anxiety, establishing connections with others, and enhancing overall psychological wellbeing.

In practice, Flego says, being more compassionate toward yourself may entail focusing on absolving yourself of blame when you make a mistake or reminding yourself that you are not alone in making errors — they are a natural part of the communal human experience. However, if your brain does not receive the information, Neff's study indicates that other people's compassion can have a comparable effect.

It's a scientific process: When you're stressed, your body needs external confirmation that the threat has passed and it's safe to return to homeostasis. Connecting with others and with yourself enables you to switch off your fear reaction and activate your prefrontal brain, allowing you to learn and grow — and ultimately be a better human.

"When we can accept our own suffering or humiliation most generously, we can really do a better job of putting ourselves in another person's place," Schwartz adds. "In that regard, shame may be an excellent teacher - it can help us develop empathy."

MEANING, ELEMENTS, CHARACTERISTICS, AND TYPES OF SOCIAL SYSTEMS

This section discusses the importance, components, characteristics, types, upkeep, and functions of social systems:

The term system connotes an organized structure, an interdependence of components. Each component has a defined location and function. Interaction between the members binds them together. To comprehend the functioning of a system, such as the human body, one must first analyze and identify the subsystems (e.g. circulatory, neural, digestive, and excretory systems) and then comprehend how these diverse subsystems interact in precise ways to carry out the body's intrinsic functions.

Similarly, society can be understood as interconnected and mutually reliant elements that work cooperatively to maintain a recognizable whole and to accomplish some purpose or goal. To put it simply, a social system is an arrangement of social interactions based on a common set of standards and values. It comprises people, each of whom has a role and a responsibility to complete.

Meaning of Social System:
Talcott Parsons is credited with popularizing the term system in contemporary sociology. The term "social system" refers to an ordered arrangement of components and their interrelationships. Each component has a defined location and function within the arrangement. Interaction between the components binds them together. Thus, a system refers to the structured interaction between constituent pieces of a structure founded on functional relationships and activates and connects these constituent parts to reality.

Society is a system of conventions, authority, and mutuality founded on the "We" sentiment and similarity. Within-society differences are not excluded. These, however, are subservient to similarity. It is based on interdependence and cooperation. It is inextricably linked via reciprocal awareness. It is fundamentally a pattern for transmitting social behavior.

It is defined by persons' reciprocal interaction and interrelationships and the structure generated by their relationships. It is not time limited. It is distinct from a collection of people and a community. According to Lapierre, "the term society does not relate to a collection of people, but to the complex pattern of norms of interaction that emerges between and among them."

In terms of society, a social system can be defined as a structure of social interactions based on shared norms and values. It comprises individuals, and each has a position and job to fulfil within it. Through this process, one influences the other; groups are created and gain influence, and countless subgroups emerge.

However, each of these is coherent. They work in unison. Individuals and groups cannot function in isolation. They are inextricably linked by shared norms and values, culture and behavior. Thus, the pattern that emerges becomes the social system.

Social systems, according to Parsons, are groups of people who interact "by shared cultural norms and meanings" in a consistent way. Individuals are the fundamental units of interaction.

According to Charles P. Loomis, the social system is built of patterned interactions amongst visual actors whose relationships are mutually oriented by forming patterns of structured and shared symbols and expectations.

Thus, all social organizations are social systems, as they are composed of interacting individuals. Each interacting member plays a role in fulfilling the position they hold in the system. For instance, parents, sons, and daughters are expected to execute particular socially recognized responsibilities or roles within the family.

Likewise, social organizations operate within the confines of a normative pattern. Thus, a social system assumes a social structure composed of distinct components that are interconnected to carry out their functions.

A social system is an all-encompassing framework. It encompasses all the varied subsystems, including economic, political, religious, and others and their interactions. Social systems are constrained by external factors such as location. And this is what distinguishes one system from another.

Elements of Social System:
The elements of the social system are as follows:

1. Beliefs and Acknowledgement:
Faiths and knowledge contribute to behavioral consistency. They serve as the governing body for several forms of human societies. The faiths or religions are the outcomes of prevailing habits and beliefs. They take pleasure in the individual's strength and are steered in a particular path.

2. Sentiment:
Man does not exist solely based on reason. Sentiments – respectful, social, and notional – have played a significant role in ensuring the continuance of society. It is inextricably related to the people's culture.

3. Purpose or objective:
Man is social and dependent from birth. He must satisfy his criteria and adhere to his commitments. Between needs and satisfactions, between end and goal, man and society exist. These factors influence the social system's nature. They paved the route for advancement and defined the receding horizons.

4. Norms and Ideals:
Society establishes specific standards and ideals to preserve the social structure and define the diverse functions of various units. These standards establish the rules and restrictions by which people or groups can achieve their cultural goals and objectives.

In other words, ideas and standards are responsible for society's ideal structure or system. They ensure that human behavior does not deviate from social norms. This results in order and stability.

5. Status-Role:
Each societal member serves a purpose. He operates based on status-role relationships. An individual may inherit it due to his birth, sex, caste, or age. It is possible to obtain it through the service given.

6. Role:
As with status, society has assigned distinct functions to various persons. Occasionally, we discover that each status is associated with a role. The role is the outward manifestation of the position. While performing particular tasks or undertaking specific activities, each individual keeps their standing in mind. This results in the social system's integration, organization, and

unity. Indeed, prestige and role are synonymous. It is impossible to disentangle them fully.

7. Power:

Conflict is a necessary component of the social system, and order is its goal. As a result, it is implicit that some should be empowered to punish the guilty and praise those who set an example. The authority exercising power varies by the group; whereas the father's authority may be ultimate in the home, the ruler's authority is supreme in the state.

8. Sanction:

It entails confirmation by the superior in the power of the subordinate's actions or the enforcement of punishment for command violations. Acts performed or not performed by established standards may result in both reward and punishment.

Social System Characteristics:

Certain traits define a social system. These attributes include the following:

1. The system is inextricably linked to the diversity of individual actors:

That is, a system or social system cannot be sustained just via the actions of a single individual. It is the product of numerous persons' actions. A system, or social system, cannot exist without the interaction of multiple persons.

2. Purpose and Objective:

Individual actors' interactions or activities should not be aimless or purposeless. These actions must be directed toward certain goals and objectives—the manifestation of many social relations by human interaction.

3. The Order and Pattern of the Constituent Units:
Simply combining diverse constituent units that originate from a social system does not always result in forming a social system. It must follow a pattern, organization, and order. The emphasized unity among numerous constituent units results in the term social system.'

4. The Basis of Unity is the Functional Relationship:
We have already seen how several constituent parts must work together to produce a system. This cohesion is founded on functional relationships. A social system is formed due to functional relationships between various constituent units.

5. Aspect of the Social System that is Physical or Environmental:
This means that each social system is bound to a specific geographical region or location, period, or society. Meaning the social system is not consistent over time, space, and circumstance. This element of the social system emphasizes its dynamic or variable nature once more.

6. Inextricably linked to the cultural system:
The social system is also inextricably related to the cultural system. This indicates that cultural systems foster unity among society's diverse members based on shared cultures, customs, and religions.

7. Expressed and implied Aims and Objects:
Additionally, the social system is linked to explicit and implicit goals. In other words, a social system is the confluence of diverse human individuals motivated by their own goals, aspirations, and wants.

8. Adjustment Characteristics:
The social system is a dynamic phenomenon that is influenced by changes in social structure. Additionally, we have seen that the social system is influenced by society's goals, objects, and wants. This suggests that the social system will remain relevant if it adapts to changing objects and requirements. It has been demonstrated that the social system changes in response to human needs, the environment, and historical events and phenomena.

9. Pattern, Order, and Balance:
A social system exhibits pattern, order, and balance. The social system is not a unified totality but a collection of distinct parts. This is coming together does not occur randomly or haphazardly. Order and chaos exist in harmony.

This is because separate units of society do not operate independently but rather within a socio-cultural pattern. Different units in the pattern perform distinct functions and roles. This indicates that the social system exhibits structure and order.

Types of Social Systems:
Parsons proposes four major social system types based on pattern variables.

1. The Particularistic Ascriptive Type:
A social system based on kinship and sociality. Assumption considerations strongly influence the normative patterns of this system. It is particularly common in preliterate societies because the primary goal is to survive biologically.

2. The Particularistic Achievement Type:
Religious concepts have a key influence in social life as a differentiating factor. When these religious beliefs are rationalized, the opportunity of developing new religious concepts arises. As a result of prophecy's inherent character, and secondly, it may be contingent on the non-empirical domain with which the porphyry is associated.

3. The Universalistic Achievement Type:
When ethical prophesy and non-empirical ideas are joined, a new set of ethical standards emerges. This is because the ethical prophet challenges the established order in the name of the supernatural. Because these standards are generated from the existing relationships, they are universalist in character. Additionally, they are linked to empirical or non-empirical aims, implying that they are goal oriented.

4. The Universalistic Ascription Type:
In this social type, ascription elements predominate overvalue orientation elements. As a result, the actor's status is emphasized above his performance. In such a system, an actor's accomplishments become almost insignificant compared to the collective aim. As a result, a system of this nature becomes political and contentious. An authoritarian state is an illustration of this sort.

The many systems of social control are responsible for the maintenance of a social system. These mechanisms ensure that the many processes of social interaction remain in balance.

Guilt Game

Signs You Might Be Suffering From Guilt
Anxiety
Crying
Insomnia
Muscle tension
Rumination
Regret
Upset stomach
Worry

My-mindguide.com

In a nutshell, these mechanisms fall under the following categories:

(1) It is via socialization that a person learns to conform to societal expectations. At birth, a child is neither social nor antisocial. However, socialization transforms him into a contributing member of society. He adapts to social conditions by adhering to social norms, ideals, and standards.

(2) Social Containment
As with socialization, social control is a system of measures used by society to shape its members' behavior to fit an established pattern of social behavior. According to Parsons, every system contains two distinct types of constituents. These are integrative and disintegrative and obstruct integration's advancement.

The Social System's Functions:
A social system is a functional configuration. It wouldn't exist if it weren't the case. A utilitarian nature helps to maintain social life. Parsons has written extensively about society's functional character. Other sociologists, such as Robert F. Bales, have also addressed the issue.

It is widely accepted that the social system faces four basic functional issues. These include the following:

1. Adaptation:
Social systems must be adaptable to changing environments. Without a doubt, a social system is the outcome of its geographical surroundings and a lengthy historical process that endows it with durability and rigidity through necessity.

Regardless, this doesn't suggest that it should be severe. It must be a malleable and functional entity.

The economy is necessary for its upkeep, division of labor is necessary for more efficient production of products and services, and role differentiation is necessary for job opportunities. Durkheim devotes much attention in the Division of Labor in Society to the effect of the division of labor and role differentiation in enabling a higher average degree of competence than would otherwise be attainable.

Lack of flexibility has frequently resulted in the social system being challenged. It sparked a revolution, resulting in the system's reorganization. The British system had shown great adaptability during the nineteenth century when the continent was engulfed in turmoil. It adapted admirably to the increasing needs of change. Over time, our system has shown an exceptional capacity for adaptation.

2. Goal Accomplishment:
Goal achievement and adaptation are inextricably linked. Both contribute to social order's upkeep.

Each social system has one or more objectives that must be accomplished cooperatively. National security is perhaps the best illustration of a societal aim. Accomplishing goals necessitates, of course, adjustment to the social and nonsocial surroundings. However, human and nonhuman resources must be mobilized effectively by the task's specific character.

For instance, there must be a procedure for ensuring that sufficient individuals, but not too many, fill each of the positions at any one moment and a method for deciding which individuals will fill which roles. Together, these procedures resolve the social system's problem of member allocation. We've already discussed the "need" for property standards. The rules governing inheritance—for example, primogeniture—partly resolve this issue.

Of course, member allocation and the distribution of scarce, valuable resources are critical for adaptability and goal attainment. The distinction between adaptability and goal accomplishment is contextual.

The economy of a society is the subsystem that produces goods and services for various purposes; the "polity," a complex society that includes most notably the government, mobilizes goods and services for achieving specific goals of the total society viewed as a single social system.

3. Integration:
A social system is an integrating system. In daily life, it is not the society but the group or subgroup in which one feels most engaged and interested. Overall, society does not factor into one's calculations. Nonetheless, as Durkheim noted, we know that the person is a product of society. Emotions, sentiments, and historical factors are all so powerful that one cannot disentangle himself from them.

These forces are most visible when society is confronted with a crisis or an external threat. A call to action on behalf of society, culture, tradition, patriotism, national solidarity, or social welfare elicits a swift reaction. Collaboration in the effort is frequently indicative of integration. It is the true foundation for integration.

In normal times, the spirit of integration is best demonstrated through adhering to regulatory standards. Failing to adhere to them will result in the domination of might over right, ego over society, and the spirit of mutuality founded on common welfare will perish. The command and obedience relationship currently exists founded on logic and order. If this is not maintained, the social order will disintegrate.

Almost every social system contains members who violate relational or regulative norms, even entire subgroups. Insofar as they meet societal criteria, violations of these standards threaten the social system.

This implies the existence of a social control system. "Social control" refers to the requirement for consistent responses to infractions to safeguard the system's integrity. When disagreements arise over the interpretation of relational or regulatory standards or on the factual aspects of conflicts of interest, agreed-upon social procedures for resolving the conflict are required. Otherwise, the social system would undergo progressive disintegration.

4. Latent Pattern-maintenance:
The essential function of a social system is to maintain patterns and regulate tensions. Without concerted effort, it is impossible to maintain and sustain social order. Indeed, every social organization contains an inherent mechanism for this purpose.

Each individual and subgroup acquires patterns as they internalize norms and values. Socialization works by imbuing actors with a suitable attitude toward rules and institutions. As a result, it's not enough to teach the actor the pattern; they must also be encouraged to follow it. This requires constant effort - in terms of social control operations.

There may still be times when the social system's components are distracted and disturbed. Tensions can occur for internal or external reasons, and society might get embroiled in a crisis. Just as distressed family marshals all available resources to overcome it, a distressed community must marshal all available resources.

This 'overcoming' phase is tension management. As with a family, society has the responsibility to maintain its member's function, alleviate their distress, and promote those who would be destructive to the system. Societies have deteriorated significantly due to the pattern maintenance and tension management mechanisms frequently failing.

Equilibrium and Social Change:
Equilibrium is a 'balanced' state. It is a "state of perfect composure." The phrase refers to the interaction of units inside a system. When systems trend toward least stress and least imbalance circumstances, an equilibrium state exists. The presence of balance between components enables the system to operate normally.

The equilibrium condition is an "integration and stable condition." It is occasionally conceivable through the development of a particular collection of productive forces, such as pressure groups, that it results in an adequate superstructure of institutions. Parsons defines equilibrium as "an ordered process of system change."

The systems for upkeeps of harmony, as indicated by him, settle two essential sorts of the cycle: "The first of these are the course of the socialization by which entertainers procure the directions important to the presentation of their parts in the social frameworks when they have not recently had them; the subsequent kind is the interaction associated with the harmony between the age of inspirations to go astray conduct and the offsetting to the rebuilding of the balanced out intuitive interaction which we have called the instrument of social control".

A social system implies order among the system's interacting units. Whether it is a balance or harmonious interpersonal connections, this order is likely to be shaken at times by social changes brought about by innovations that compel new notions of roles and standards. When a woman works away from home, her job as a housewife changes; this shift is certain to affect other social institutions as well.

Maintaining the order of a social system is challenging when social changes occur frequently. In the equilibrium/disequilibrium analysis, Herbert Spencer proposed cause and effect links to explain the changing character of societies.

The structural-functional pattern of the institutions that comprise a society would alter in response to changes in the external environment and its internal conditions. The disposition of the components of society would change until a suitable 'equilibrium' is attained.

Spencer's development of the equilibrium theory demonstrated its universal application. He emphasized that individuals of a community are always adapting to its material substance. "Each society demonstrates the equilibration process by the ongoing adjustment of its population to its means of subsistence," he said.

A tribe of humanity subsisting on wild animals and fruits is like any tribe of inferior species, constantly swinging between the maximum and minimum numbers the location can support. Though artificial production is perpetually enhanced, a superior race constantly modifies the limit on population imposed by external factors, and there is always a check on the population at the temporary limit attained".

Spencer developed his theory of equilibrium by referring to numerous economic features and the industrial system of a society that is always adjusting to the forces of supply and demand.' Additionally, he has discussed political institutions in terms of 'equilibrium-disequilibrium'. It is equally applicable to all societies.

Equilibrium-disequilibrium adjustments can explain the changes in society as a whole and its interactions with its constituents. According to Ronald Fletcher's The Making of Sociology, "Marxian Historical Materialism" is an "equilibrium-disequilibrium analysis of historical sequences of social order and change, and an explanation of this process in terms of material changes, accompanying social conflict, and its resolution."

Guilt Game

My-mindguide.com

FAMILY ESTRANGEMENT'S SHAME AND GUILT

Why do we internalize our decision to close ties with our family?

Human beings are social creatures. Our families are the first places where we can identify ourselves with others.

If we are fortunate, we are born into a family that gives both a healthy level of protection from the outside world and a healthy status of connection to it.

Regrettably, some people have an entirely different perspective on family. Rather than providing us with the secure cocoon, we seek, those closest to us are emotionally, physically, or sexually abusive. They live in fear of doing or saying the wrong thing and struggle to maintain a neutral posture among family strife. Living in a terrified and silent household takes a toll on your mental and physical health, to the point that the only option sometimes appears to be to cut off all relationships altogether.

Most people make this choice solely to avoid remaining trapped in a harmful environment. Most persons who have been estranged from a loved one also feel a deep sense of shame and guilt.

You may find yourself looking around at happy mothers and daughters, brothers, sons, and fathers and wondering, Was I correct to do what I did when it resulted in this outcome? Whatever precipitated the alienation, it's natural to feel some remorse about it. When we're separated from our family, it's common to feel guilty because we assume we've done something wrong. Interestingly, suppose a friend or coworker expressed their unhappiness with being a member of their family. In that case, you might believe they were justified in withdrawing, but it's challenging to maintain a rational viewpoint when it comes to oneself.

Another prevalent emotion is a shame. Unlike guilt, which is a sense that we've done something wrong, shame is a self-judgment that our entire being is flawed. What is truly wrong with me that prevents me from having a deep, healthy relationship with my family? "The family" is frequently depicted as a sacred entity. Even when there is fallout in the movies, there is always a deathbed reunion. We envision large families as cheerful, boisterous, supporting situations, and we presume that mothers and fathers have their children's best interests at heart. If "blood is thicker than water," what about me is so faulty that my blood has become profoundly toxic?

While guilt is never pleasant, the sense that you have done something wrong is probably more manageable than the sense that something is wrong with you. The shame associated with familial alienation pervades your core and can tremendously affect your self-esteem. During my brief reunion with my family — which lasted only a few months after years of alienation — I felt relieved to bring up my brother and sister in conversation. Although I had resolved my alienation issues, it was still a relief to be a "regular" family member again. It was comforting to believe that I was a person who got along well with all my siblings.

When my efforts to maintain friendly relations with my brother and my sister failed (I retained good relations with another sister and my mother), shame and guilt became my go-to locations. I realized that my constant self-questioning was far more intense than any sentiments of grief for my siblings. "Am I simply an evil person?" I asked my wife?.

Despite my years of awareness, I was judging myself from an emotionally scarred place—and my assessment was distorted by our society's ideas of "the family."

If you find yourself deciding to isolate yourself, keep the following in mind: Your family may consist of siblings, parents, and children, but they are also individuals. They have no right to dupe you into believing their acts are justified when in fact, they are abusive. They have no claim on you simply because you are related to them.

If you are a member of a family when the only alternative feels like estrangement, it is awful, and nobody wishes to be in that circumstance. However, it is your choice, and taking that path does not automatically make you a bad or misguided person. After coming to terms with estrangement, most people discover a sense of serenity and relief that was previously impossible while being a member of their toxic family and can begin the process of healing.

DO YOU FEEL GUILTY ABOUT YOUR PARENTAL RELATIONSHIP? UTILIZE THIS METHOD

One thing never fails to astound me. It is the percentage of decent, caring people who experience unexplained guilt in their relationships with their parents.

Indeed, as an Expert of the unconscious mind , I have witnessed this so frequently that it has inspired me to conduct much thought and research on the sources of these guilty sentiments. And my concerns about this played a significant role in my decision to write my second book on this topic.

Today's essay contains an excerpt from the book, somewhat condensed and edited. I hope it assists you in identifying the roots of your guilt, determining whether your guilt is beneficial to you, and determining what you can do about it.

Your Relationship With Your Parents

Our brains are wired with an innate desire for our parents' attention and understanding. As with necessary vitamins and minerals, we must get an adequate supply of these fundamental emotional elements to develop into strong, self-assured, and emotionally adept adults.

We did not choose to have these requirements, and we will never eliminate them. They are strong and real, and they propel us on in life.

Nonetheless, legions of children grow up receiving, at best, a watered-down version of their parent's attention, understanding, and acceptance. I refer to this failure to provide a child's basic emotional requirements as Childhood Emotional Neglect, or CEN.

Many people attempt to minimize these fundamental criteria by framing them as a flaw or by declaring themselves to be exempt from them.

I am unconcerned about what my folks think of me.
I'm sick of attempting to please them.
They simply no longer matter to me.

I completely see why you would convince yourself that your most fundamental emotional demands are unreal. After all, it's excruciating to have your most fundamental biological and personal needs thwarted throughout your youth. It's a normal coping mechanism to lessen or eliminate that irritation, grief, and unhappiness.

However, the reality is that NO ONE, and I mean NO ONE, is immune to this desire. You can push it down, deny it, or delude yourself, but it will not disappear. That is why growing up in an environment where you are not seen, known, understood, or approved by your parents affects you.

Once adults, in addition to the impacts of Emotional Neglect (which are discussed in previous sections), certain paradoxical feelings plague CEN children's relationships with their parents.

Numerous emotionally deprived youngsters grow up in seemingly normal environments. They may have had appropriate housing, adequate education, and met all of their fundamental wants. Yet their most fundamental emotional needs are gradually and covertly thwarted.

As adults, CEN individuals recall all the materialistic gifts their parents gave them but are frequently oblivious of the significance of their parents' emotional failures. As a result, CEN children have extremely complicated and perplexing feelings regarding their parents.

Typically, love and rage coexist, appreciation and deprivation coexist, and compassion coexists with impatience or boredom. You may feel guilty for wondering why you do not feel your parents' better and loving thoughts. Guilt appears out of nowhere or for perplexing reasons. And you have no understanding of any of these emotions.

Growing up in this manner is not a guarantee of being harmed. Indeed, it is quite doable if, rather than denying it, you acknowledge that your demands are natural and legitimate. Then you may control your emotional demands and your feelings on a deliberate basis. In this manner, you can alleviate the suffering associated with growing up unnoticed, unrecognized, or misunderstood.

The Guilt

Do you find yourself becoming irrationally furious at your parents when you engage with them, only to feel bad later? Are you required to attend family events merely because you've always done so and your parents expect you to? Would you feel very bad if you wanted to make a healthier and more beneficial change? I'm guessing the answer to one or more of those questions is yes.

However, you must recognize that guilt is ineffective in instances like these. Guilt is intended to deter us from harming or violating others. It is not intended to prevent us from defending ourselves. You, who simply need to look after yourself and avoid being continually harmed or neglected (or both), are the last ones who should feel guilty.

Your guilt may surface and obstruct your efforts to make healthy adjustments and improve your self-protection. Your guilt is depleting, and it increases your vulnerability to more injury. That is why it must be fought back. I created the strategy outlined below to assist you in precisely doing that. Additionally, you can utilize it in any other situation when unproductive guilt plagues or weighs you down.

The Four-Step Guilt Management Method

1. Rate your level of guilt on a scale of 1 to 10, with 1 reflecting no guilt at all and 10 representing the largest amount.

2. Assign your blame to its legitimate cause. To accomplish this, ask yourself the following helpful questions and jot down your responses.

- For what specifically do I feel guilty?

- How much of my guilt stems from an action I took or am considering taking, and how much stems from an emotion I am experiencing, such as anger, resentment, irritation, or repulsion?

- Is my guilt communicating with me in any way? For instance, is it advising me to alter my behavior?

- Are my parents (or siblings, or spouse) attempting to instill guilt in me?

3. Make some judgments based on your assessment of guilt and attributions. If your shame is not communicating anything beneficial to you, attempt to control it actively so

that it does not impair your capacity to set boundaries with your parents. This should be straightforward if your rating is low. If it is a medium, you may find yourself frequently pausing to remind yourself that your guilt is unproductive. If it is excessive, I strongly advise you to speak with someone about it. You may wish to seek the assistance of a knowledgeable specialist. I've witnessed guilt paralyze many capable individuals, preventing them from making important changes in their relationships with their parents.

4. Use these reminders to help you cope with your guilt. Reread this list as needed.

- A lot of what you're feeling about your parents is understandable. There is a reason why you have them.

- You have no control over how you feel.

- Feelings are not terrible or wrong in and of themselves. Only actions may be judged in this manner, and only actions can be judged.

- The emotional scars left by your parents' refusal to validate you will remain no matter how much money they provide you.

- Setting boundaries with your parents is essential for your well-being and the well-being of your family. Even if you don't want to, this is true.

Guilt has an incredible ability to divert your attention from more helpful emotions, such as anger. Your thoughts of rage toward your parents are justified.

Is your anger advising you to take a step back from your parents? To better defend yourself? To discuss CEN with your parents? To establish boundaries with your parents? To refuse to fulfil a familial obligation? To increase your emotional distance from your parents today? All these messages are quite valuable to you, and they are obliterated when guilt enters the picture.

Your feelings are valid and necessary. However, guilt is not beneficial to you. It is up to you to control your guilt to own, listen to, and regulate all your other emotions. Then, and only then, will your relationship with your parents make sense to you.

EXPLORING GUILT IN FAMILY BUSINESS

In my consulting business we frequently speak with family members who have become emotionally conflicted by guilt in our work with business-owning families. They may feel guilty about their prosperity at a time when others are suffering; they may feel ongoing guilt about inheriting the fruits of their parents' or grandparents' hard work; they may feel guilty about opportunities given to them rather than to other family members, or they may express guilt about taking over management positions previously held by senior generation members. Our customers frequently describe these and numerous other examples of the distressing experience of a guilty conscience.

Multiple layers of relationships link members of a family company. They may take on the role of a boss one minute and a father the next; a board member one day and a sister the next; a mother on one phone call and a shareholder the next. In each of these combinations, the fundamental connection needs of each of us interplay in a complex way. A "guilty conscience" experience regulates three primary wants:

- The need to belong, to be welcomed and united with loved ones.

- The requirement to preserve a balance of giving and taking and arrive at a fair equilibrium through a continual process of exchange.

- The desire for predictability and safety, as well as for order in social convention, which is frequently fine-tuned over years of learning "how things are done around here."

It's beneficial to recognize that the experience of guilt or innocence is a critical tool for navigating between various needs, particularly when confronted with difficult decisions. The "conscience" functions similarly to an internal organ that constantly judges between what benefits and what harms relationships. Just as the eye is always experiencing light and dark, our conscience employs feelings of guilt or innocence to track how we feel in each of our interactions and when conflicting loyalties result in us feeling guilty and innocent. What makes a daughter feel innocent in the presence of her parents may cause her to feel guilty in the presence of her husband. What makes a brother feel innocent during an emergency financial meeting with his sibling stockholders may make him feel guilty as a manager addressing layoff options. When family members balance their demands with the needs of others, family business systems and relationships thrive.

Our desires to belong, strike a balance between giving and taking, and keep inside the boundaries of social convention all contribute to the survival of the family business structure. However, each need has its own distinct goals and associated feelings of guilt and innocence.

When an action threatens one's belonging, guilt feels like exclusion and fear of estrangement. When we act in ways that promote belonging, we experience naivety as deep inclusion and closeness, even if it may cause harm to individuals outside the group. When the group's purpose shifts, the "rules" controlling acceptable behavior shift, and what supports one group often makes another feel guilty.

If you don't give and you don't receive equally, you'll feel like you've done something wrong. When we are in equilibrium, we experience innocence as completeness or freedom. Giving more than one receives can make one feel powerful and entitled, while the receiver frequently feels obligated in this transaction.

Guilt is experienced as transgression or fear of repercussions when one violates a group's social rules. The sense of innocence about group standards can show loyalty or commitment, even while the consequences for individuals outside the group may be severe.

HOW UNDERSTANDING GUILT AND SHAME CAN AID OUR CROSS-CULTURAL WITNESS

Modern missiologists frequently compel missionaries to choose between a "guilt-innocence" gospel and a message of "honor-shame." However, guilt and shame are inextricably linked.

"What happened, and is everyone all right?"

That important question has been a constant companion throughout your parenting journey if you're a parent. A glass breaking and your child is crying alert you to the fact that something has gone wrong.

Likewise, it does not take much intellect or research to recognize that our world is broken and in desperate need of assistance. We witness others' suffering, experience our own, and yearn for respite, escape, and tranquility. How do we diagnose and explain to a world that is desperately seeking solutions to escape its brokenness as for example in the Christian faith there the good news of Christ?

God's common kindness bestows upon us emotions—truly a part of our moral conscience—that reveal two ways in which we are spiritually ruined. Christians believe that the realities of guilt and shame are God's gracious provision for bringing our brokenness and dependence on him to light. Additionally, They strongly believe that knowing the gospel's relationship to guilt and shame enables us to honestly deliver the gospel in language relevant to our society and other global contexts.

Guilt is concerned with an individual's legal status before the law. A judge renders a legal judgment based on evidence that an individual has violated the law. In an ideal world, Guilt is an unbiased assessment of one's compliance with the law. Because sin is a violation of God's sacred rule, justice must be served. Guilt is a legal status that should elicit moral feelings because of our relationship with the law.

Again referring to the Christian belief: by his ideal, substitutionary penance on the cross, God covered our transgression and paid for our obligation, along these lines liberating us from our wrongdoing related responsibility. By contrast, shame is concerned with interpersonal relationships within the family. When children maintain polite, obedient relationships with their parents, they get honor. From a shame perspective, sin is the act of ending a connection, dishonoring the family and defying the family's authoritative figure. Disgrace falls on the individual, their family, their community, and the authority/elder/father of the group when this relationship is severed.

To be delivered from our humiliation, we must be adopted into God's family and transformed into loving children rather than rebellious enemies.

"Guilt is a legal issue, whereas shame is a relational issue. The gospel offers both legal and relational redemption."

In summary, guilt is a legal issue, whereas shame is a relational issue. The gospel offers both legal and relational redemption.

Again referring to the Christian belief, a gospel presentation that emphasizes guilt would describe the law, our failure to obey it, the consequence for our sin, the impending judgment, and Jesus' perfect sacrifice. Salvation alters our legal standing immediately, as we are justified—declared righteous. Christ's fulfilment of the law and payment of the penalty for our sin is the basis for our justification and redemption. We receive Christ's righteousness, and Christ bears the burden of our sin. The Father absolves sinners of guilt because he is satisfied with His Son's work on the cross.

A gospel presentation emphasizing shame would help understand our relationship with God in the garden and how sin shattered that perfect relationship. Adam and Eve experienced shame and were immediately aware of their nakedness due to their sin. They were publicly exposed physically and spiritually as creatures who had disobeyed their Creator. When we defy the will of God, we dishonor and disrespect him because of our rebellion. Our sin has provided Satan with an opportunity to boast and defame the name of God.

Additionally, a gospel conversation focusing on shame would discuss the restoration of this connection and emphasize the Father's love, grace, and forgiveness. By sending Jesus, the Father has accomplished all that is necessary to bring glory to his name (reversal of shame) and fully integrate us into his kingdom family. This adoption occurs as sons and daughters, not as servants or enslaved people. These themes of relational breakdown and healing frequently strike a more powerful chord with persons living in shame-based cultures worldwide.

Since they illustrate significant consequences of sin and the Fall, both guilt and shame should be addressed in full gospel presentations.

Western Christians should be conscious that our tendency to emphasize sin's guilt comes from our culture's emphasis on individualism. When contextualizing the gospel—particularly in cross-cultural situations—it is prudent to understand the people's worldview and tailor gospel presentations to fit cultural concerns and perceived needs. A faithful presentation would address the issues raised by Scripture that may be a blind spot in that same society.

Both guilt and shame are necessary components of comprehending the human need for redemption and cannot be highlighted at the expense of the other. Guilt serves as a reminder of our need for redemption, while shame serves as a reminder of our need for reconciliation. In this context, at the cross, both redemption and reconciliation are granted!

THE GIFT OF GUILT

Utilizing Eastern philosophy to aid in the eradication of guilt

"It would be difficult to assert that guilt is an egoistic paralysis that has no basis or outcome, but it would be equally difficult to assert the opposite. As I think on this section, I am motivated by Eastern wisdom to describe how we can recognize and overcome our shame."

Guilt offers no solutions and keeps us stuck in our current identities. That does not imply that we should feel bad for feeling guilty, but it is also pointless to fight guilt when it appears—replacing one conflict with another is a self-defeating routine. So what are we to do?

Guilt is a paralysis of the ego.
I've felt guilty when I didn't know how to feel anything else. I was at a loss for what else to do for myself, and while this is my issue, I was also unable to help others in greatest need. I concluded that shame is only an internal projection of oneself, but it is far from a straightforward solution to a problem—it is a paralyzing selfish emotion. It hinders us from progressing until we recognize its futility, which occurs only after developing other characteristics.

Before beginning this process of guilt disintegration, we must understand the source of this emotion. It begins with distancing and our capacity to identify guilt by assigning it a label — for example, by mentally writing "guilt" on a piece of paper—a means of being truthful to ourselves.

Breaking down emotion

When guilt manifests and takes hold, the reasons are numerous. For instance, an outsider may have sown a seed of guilt in our minds in the past or present. It is very likely, but we are accountable for allowing it to grow. Furthermore, when we are confronted with the source of our guilt, the resulting immobility is readily apparent: our self-image is devalued, if not demonized, in our efforts to achieve a feeling of justice or justice-centered in a desire to experience this shame. It's a vicious circle: one considers just one's interests but feels bad for injuring others.

The antithesis of responsibility

I misbehaved with someone close to me nine months ago and became more furious than I'd ever been. I spent the next three months feeling guilty, which kept me from coming to any conclusions and from properly comprehending what had occurred. Like all negative thoughts, guilt obscures one's face and impairs one's ability to observe a situation objectively. Therefore, why do we consider ourselves to be our judges?

It is, like shame, an egotistical process. Shame and guilt are frequently linked and have comparable consequences: worsening one's self-image, obsession with oneself, and neglect of people we have injured. Guilt is so excessive that Tibetans have no words for it. It is just the outcome of too much shame attached to our own past behaviors that others deemed undesirable. Once this stigma is internalized, it takes on the form of guilt. Guilt is, in the end, the opposite of accountability and represents a dualistic worldview, which renders it erroneous, simply because there is no global judge to declare that the dualistic worldview is pragmatic, etc.

Guilt is a mere symptom.

It is a simple but necessary reminder that shame is the outcome of anxiety of not living up to expectations or achieving the demands of behavioral success imposed by... ourselves. As a result, we must let go. To eliminate guilt, we must replace it with moral responsibility, including refusing to accept responsibility. However, responsibility enables us to learn about ourselves, improve, and avoid seeing our emotions appear in our brains.

The practice of compassion

Whether verbal, mental, or physical, our acts can have a detrimental influence on others, thereby causing our guilt. Responsibility enables us to reflect on how we aim to improve ourselves for the benefit of others.

In Buddhism, the practice of mett-Bhavana, or universal love meditation, provides a technique to transcend guilt constructively for oneself and others. It begins with our capacity to befriend ourselves. According to Buddha, you can look for someone more deserving of love and affection than you, but you will never find him. You are equally deserving of this love and affection.

To be eradicated from guilt, it must be positively perceived.

The capacity to develop compassion for oneself and the recognition that, like other persons, you do not have complete control over the repercussions of all your acts due to ignorance results in an awareness that you are not worse than others.

Thus, we can view shame as a manifestation of our desire to better and change ways that we do not wish to. For instance, I discovered that I was allowing the disapproving gazes of particular loved ones to dwell in my thoughts and obstruct my progress. When one understands guilt, it becomes a helpful indicator of our choices to be free and happy—the only thing we deserve.

GUILT'S EFFECT ON RELATIONSHIPS

To my surprise, the clerk pointed out the Tiger Woods cover as I was about to pay for an cheese sandwich and a newspaper at the convenience store. Is he truly feeling bad, or is he attempting to elicit pity from his wife and others?

I'm not sure, I responded, unsure whether it was time to go on to another deli. It's tricky in terms of guilt and connections. I don't believe it's simple.

Numerous people, it appears, were asking the same question and were compiling data about it. When HCD Research evaluated Tigers apology evaluations, they discovered that men and women assessed his sincerity similarly, with 61% of women and 58% of men believing he was honest. Apart from whatever happens to Tiger Woods, this raises many issues with guilt in relationships: What exactly is it? Why do people experience this? What does an apology entail?

Anyone who has ever had a sense of guilt over breaking a moral standard and accepted responsibility for it will understand what it means to feel that way. Regarding guilt, there are several theories out there to consider. For example, early Freudian thinking linked guilt to sexual impulses or moral prohibitions against sexual desires. From this vantage point, guilt entails internal self-judgment.

An Interpersonal Perspective

A unique and essential viewpoint on understanding guilt in relationships is provided by Roy Braumeister, Arlene Stillwell, and Todd Heatherton's 1994 essay Guilt: An Interpersonal Approach, published in the journal Psychological Bulletin. They define shame as the discomfort we experience when we cause another person harm through a violation or an unfairness. They observe that, while guilt can be directed at anybody, it is most intense in close personal connections, which are defined by expectations of mutual concern, trust, and love. In a personal connection, for example, lying, refusing to assist, disregarding the other's requests, or proof of an affair are all likely to result in more anguish and guilt.

From an interpersonal standpoint, guilt is induced by two factors: empathy for our partner's suffering and fear that the transgression will result in rejection or the end of the relationship. Frequently, the apology is the attempted and anticipated dynamic of mending.

However, because couples live in a unique and complicated world, guilt is experienced and expressed differently. An apology can take on a variety of shapes with varying implications.

Take the following into consideration:

Self-Righting Guilt

It frequently occurs in relationships when partners know that what they are doing or not doing is badly affecting their other, prompting some guilt and a change in habit or behavior. Here are a few illustrations:

Observing his wife's weary expression, he recognizes that she has been the one waking up with the baby nine times out of ten and advises that they exchange night shifts.

Or

Recognizing that he is visibly anxious about visiting his mother in the nursing home, she knows that declining to accompany him would deprive him of much-needed support, so she volunteers to accompany him.

In such circumstances, additional dialogue and an admission of guilt are frequently withheld or deemed unnecessary.

Induced Guilt

Guilt can be produced in partners due to a partner's self-expression of needs or because of deliberate manipulation.

Self-Expression

Making needs known is a necessary component of productive communication between partners. While it is necessary to explain to a partner that they are causing suffering (intentionally or unintentionally), the message is likely to elicit some remorse. Due to the unpleasant nature of guilt, many spouses respond with an initial knee-jerk response. They withdraw into silence, ignore the other person's emotions, or behave defensively in some way. For instance, she says: I understand that you enjoy networking with our friends, but the way you flatter other ladies in front of me makes me feel humiliated.

He responds:

So now I'm obliged to monitor every word I utter?

When you come to this stage in the conversation, you hope that your partners have the endurance to continue the conversation past the first two lines and find a better spot. Hopefully, she persists long enough to be heard, and he is receptive.

She says:

I adore how outgoing you are. I'm attempting to convey that it's difficult to feel unique and desirable when you're always admiring other ladies in front of me.

He responds silently and exits the room. He returns.

I'm sorry. I understand.

While experiencing guilt resulting from your partner's declaration of need might be challenging, it can serve as a point of self-reflection that promotes mutual communication and pair bonding.

Manipulation To guilt them into it.

Inducing guilt in a spouse to elicit specific behavior, maintain power, or punish a partner is a toxic marital dynamic. It frequently includes the following lines:

You need to spend more time with the children; they sense your lack of affection.

I take care of everything for you, and you take care of nothing for me.

I'll never forget what you did to us when you lost the business money.

Certain partners will react angrily to the instilled guilt. Others will succumb to resentment, even if they are not responsible. Certain individuals will internalize the repeated reminders of their transgression in a way that undermines their self-esteem.

In any event, generating guilt intentionally is detrimental to a relationship. It deprives a couple of the potential of honestly experiencing guilt and using it as a signal of concern and a catalyst for change.

IS GUILT TAKING OVER YOUR LIFE?

Is your guilty conscience following you about, wondering how you could have done more or more for your partner, your children, your community, or your career? Where does such paralyzing guilt originate? How much of a toll does it exact on you? And, maybe most crucially, how are you going to shake it? Continue reading to learn more. Also, don't feel bad about spending time on yourself.

The range of guilt experienced by individuals is wide. "Certain folks lack the good guilt that keeps you on track. Others suffer from crippling remorse that eats away at their souls; they rarely have moments of calm, "According to Michael McKee, PhD, vice chairman of The Cleveland Clinic's department of psychiatry and psychology.

Why do some people allow remorse to torment them? According to experts, personality is partial to a fault.

"Timid, insecure persons may suffer from excessive guilt and constantly second guessing' of themselves and their behaviors," explains Patricia Farrell, PhD, clinical psychologist and author of How to be Your Therapist: A Step-by-Step Guide to Developing a Competent, Confident Life.

"People who have an obsessive-compulsive or obsessive personality disorder, or who exhibit these personality features, are also prone to excessive rumination about their behaviors, which increases their guilt quotient," she says.

The Social Factors That Contribute to Guilt

While individuals' personalities may predispose them to guilt, social norms also play a role.

Males and females alike receive strong signals about "gender-specific" expectations that, when not met, might result in guilt.

"Women develop self-esteem as a result of their relationships", Mary Ann Bauman, MD, director of Women's Health for INTEGRIS, an Oklahoma-based nonprofit health system, explains.

Men and their Guilt

Men, on the other hand, are raised with distinct expectations. "Men develop self-esteem as a result of their accomplishments," Bauman explains. Thus, a man who does not develop into the athlete or scholar that he or his parents expected is frequently plagued by guilt. A child's need to be accepted by their parents is very acute.

"I have patients who are college students who wish to major in x, y, or z but tell me, 'My father is a physician and wishes for me to follow in his footsteps,'" says Kiki Weingarten, executive director of DailyLifeConsulting.com.

Parenthood also creates avenues for guilt. "It is not just working parents; it is all parents. They may feel as though they should be doing more. They're peering over their neighbors' shoulders, believing they're accomplishing more "Naomi Drew is a parenting specialist and author located in New Jersey.

Even as we approach our golden years, the propensity for guilt might persist.

Consider the case of parents who enter a nursing facility. "They frequently feel really bad about the cost, knowing they must sell everything to pay for the nursing home rather than passing it on to their children," says Barbara Ensor, PhD, a psychologist at Stella Maris, a Baltimore long-term care facility.

Meanwhile, the children of these parents frequently experience shame as well. "Many family members feel bad about having to place their mother in a nursing home and being unable to care for her," Ensor explains.

Guilt's Negative Consequences

The overwhelming sensation of guilt is detrimental to both our mental and physical health.

"If you're feeling guilty, you're stressed. If your body produces stress-related hormones, you put yourself at risk for mild ailments such as headaches and backaches, "McKee explains to WebMD. That is not all. "Additionally, it [guilt] adds to cardiovascular disease and digestive issues. Over time, it may even have a detrimental effect on the immune system, "McKee asserts.

Allowing Excessive Guilt to Go

If you feel guilty as an adult, the likelihood is that the negative feelings began in childhood, and it may take some time to untangle all the suffocating layers of it. However, it is possible.

Rehearse, saying no. "As with any change, there will be discomfort," Weingarten says. However, it is possible and necessary, particularly if you continuously place yourself last.

However, what if you have difficulty saying no? "Ask yourself why you're afraid to say no,'" Weingarten advises. "It's possible that you are worried about not being liked. That other will gossip about you behind your back?" This should assist you in putting your worry into context.

Bear in mind to look after yourself. " Consider the following: 'What is sufficient? How am I to manage all of these tasks without collapsing?' Because when you come apart, you are detrimental to everyone. "You absolutely must look after yourself."

Building on Success

Begin by making minor changes to your habits. When you first say 'no,' you will have some insecurities. It becomes easier as you amass a portfolio of successes.

Your expectations should be re-evaluated. "Assess your successes, or lack thereof, and determine whether they are the correct ones for you," Bauman recommends. "At times, we are moved to act in certain ways because it was the correct thing to do for our parents. However, your parents' circumstances were not your own. "She serves as a reminder.

Identify the source of that guilty voice. "If it is your mother's or father's, I implore people to relinquish it.

"Reduce your expectations," Natalie Gahrmann, a life coach and founder of N-R-G Coaching Associates, advises. For instance, if you're attempting to arrive on time for a meeting and feel terrible about arriving a few minutes late, consider the alternative: you speed and receive a citation, or you cause an accident. Being a few minutes late is not inexcusable.

Put an end to your shame over making errors—view errors as a learning opportunity, not evidence that you are a bad, lazy person.

WHY ARE SHAME AND GUILT IMPORTANT TO MENTAL HEALTH?

Shame and guilt are two self-conscious feelings that almost everyone experiences.

These are typically negative feelings that cause someone to feel horrible about themselves and have undesirable repercussions. Shame and guilt are critical emotional components of living a prosocial lifestyle.

This section will examine several psychological ideas regarding emotions, internal and external feelings of shame and guilt, and lastly, strategies for overcoming guilt and shame to avoid harmful self-evaluations. To begin, it's critical to distinguish between shame and guilt, two self-conscious emotions that are comparable yet significantly distinct.

Before you continue, we thought you would enjoy free access to our three self-compassion exercises. These precise, science-based exercises will not only help you develop your compassion and kindness but will also equip you to help your clients, students, or workers show themselves more compassion.

Defending Against Misconceptions: Shame vs Guilt
The following characteristics characterize both guilt and shame:

"negative affective states that emerge in response to a transgression or weakness; both are self-conscious emotions, requiring self-reflection to manifest.

This explains why they are frequently confused, an issue exacerbated by the fact that one might simultaneously feel shame and guilt. One effective and widely recognized framework separates the two by stating that "[s]hame is about the self," whereas "guilt is about the real-world—actions or inactions, events for which one bears responsibility."

Someone who feels guilty regrets a particular behavior, whereas someone who feels shame regrets some component of their personality. This is occasionally referred to as the "self-behavior difference." According to this argument, it is far easier to lessen guilt than alleviate shame because atoning for poor behavior is far easier than radically changing oneself.

Indeed, an examination of the brain correlates of guilt and shame (as well as embarrassment) discovered that the neurological underpinnings of guilt and shame were similar yet distinct, showing that while the two emotions have some common ground, they are essentially distinct.

This essay will generally adhere to Lewis's (1971) concept of shame and guilt. When someone feels horrible about themselves as a person because of mistreatment, they are suffering from shame. On the other hand, when someone feels awful about their behavior, they are experiencing guilt. While this framework is widely recognized, it is worthwhile to consider other perspectives regarding the two emotions.

Behavioral Psychology and Additional Theories About Guilt and Shame

Earlier conceptualizations of shame and guilt asserted that shame is a public experience (induced by others' reactions), but guilt is a private sensation (caused by internal conflict about morality).

However, this model is not frequently maintained by contemporary philosophers, as evidence indicates that both shame and guilt are experienced at comparable rates in public and private.

Indeed, Lewis's framework (1971) runs counter to the idea of shame being public and guilt being private, as Lewis asserts that shame is aimed inwardly at the self, but guilt is focused outwards at one's behaviors or acts.

These "self-blaming" emotions are vital to the development of interpersonal relationships because they promote a balance between an individual's urges and the rights and wants of others, according to certain definitions of shame and guilt.

While acknowledging the relevance of shame and guilt, this is an important point to express. When a genuine wrong is committed, feelings of shame and remorse are the first step toward repairing the harm.

According to some contemporary critics, there are two distinct sorts of guilt: "maladaptive, neurotic guilt" and "adaptive, prosocial guilt." These researchers claim that the type of guilt analyzed is contingent on the measure utilized and that future studies should differentiate between these two types of guilt.

The researchers distinguished guilt into "checklist guilt," which is quantified by asking individuals about prior experiences with guilt, and "scenario guilt," which is quantified by asking people about hypothetical guilt they might encounter in future scenarios.

This divergence may also help to explain why shame is widely accepted as detrimental, although guilt has not been definitively proven as either adaptive or maladaptive. According to the rationale of this research (which, as the authors admit, need additional investigation), adaptive guilt is guilt directed toward doing the right thing in the future. In contrast, maladaptive guilt is remorse directed toward the past.

Finally, shame and guilt are social feelings designed to deter people from acting only in their self-interest. As we shall see, shame is a predominantly maladaptive feeling, whereas guilt is a predominantly adaptive emotion. This divergence is evident in both internal and exterior emotional manifestations.

Guilt and Shame: A Psychological Experience

One study investigated the psychological processes that resulted in guilt being classified as a prosocial emotion. The researchers discovered that when people are guilty, they pay greater attention to "reparatory stimuli," such as the terms "assist," "apologize," and "repair," than to other sorts of stimuli.

Notably, these researchers discovered that guilt increased individuals' favorable feelings about these reparatory stimuli, making them more appealing.

In other words, this study discovered that shame motivated people to pay greater attention to prosocial, reparatory thoughts and to feel better about them.

Another study investigated guilt's prosocial function in moral comparisons. These researchers discovered that when participants were encouraged to recall instances in their daily lives where someone was more moral than them (for example, if someone gave up their bus seat for an older adult but the participant did not), they felt terrible.

However, they found that this remorse had a prosocial effect, encouraging participants to act more morally in the future. These studies demonstrate the prosocial function of self-conscious emotions such as guilt in people's daily lives and the psychological mechanisms that contribute to guilt being a prosocial emotion.

A meta-analysis of the literature on shame discovered that the prevalent perspective (that shame is always antisocial and results in avoidance) is unsatisfactory. This meta-analysis established that shame does result in avoidance and antisocial behavior in specific circumstances where the damage appears irreversible. When the damage is reversible, shame, on the other hand, can motivate the same prosocial and constructive activities as guilt.

In other words, in less catastrophic situations when damage may be repaired, guilt and shame both make a person feel awful and push them to correct the problem to feel better.

However, in more serious instances, where the harm appears to be irreversible, guilt and shame both make a person feel horrible, but only guilt encourages the individual to repair the damage (or as much of it as possible). In contrast, shame motivates the individual to avoid the damage. This implies that shame is as prosocial as guilt in some but not all contexts,

Guilt and humiliation are common reactions to having done something wrong. One major difference between the two is that while shame makes you feel bad about yourself, guilt makes you do better morally because it makes you want to feel better about yourself (albeit, in certain circumstances, disgrace may likewise push individuals to act in a more upright manner).

While shame and guilt are experienced mentally differently, they are also exhibited behaviorally differently.

The Functionalism Of Self-Conscious Emotions

One study examined people's reactions to guilt, humiliation, and anger and discovered some surprising findings.

They discovered that individuals experiencing shame were more likely to avoid eye contact than individuals experiencing guilt. Additionally, they discovered that individuals experiencing guilt were more inclined to wish to remedy whatever damage they may have caused than individuals experiencing shame. To sum up, researchers have found that:

"shame is defined by the desire to conceal and flee, while guilt is defined by the desire to repair."

This result has been observed in youngsters as young as two. One study convinced children that they had broken an adult's toy and assessed whether the child felt shame or remorse behaviorally.

These researchers discovered that children who felt shame acted antisocially, avoiding the adult's gaze or concealing the toy. Still, children who felt remorse acted prosaically, swiftly informing the adult of their actions and attempting to repair the object as best they could.

This demonstrates that guilt and shame act similarly in toddlers and adults. Indeed, the authors assert that:

"[g]uilt may even play a mechanical function in the development of prosocial behavior by establishing itself as a critical part of children's conscience."

Another study evaluated athletes' self-handicapping, which occurs when an individual sabotages their preparation for a tense performance to blame the performance on the preparation.

For instance, someone concerned about a test they must take may avoid preparing for the test, reasoning that if they receive a low mark, it is because they did not study.

The self-handicapping study discovered that athletes who are more susceptible to shame are more likely to self-handicap. In contrast, those who are more susceptible to guilt are less likely to self-handicap.

Another study investigated the connection between guilt, shame, and alcohol usage. The authors discovered that shame-prone individuals had greater difficulty controlling their drinking, which resulted in increased consumption. In contrast, guilt-prone individuals had more control over their drinking, which resulted in decreased consumption. Another way to put it is in line with the idea that shame motivates people to hide and escape.

By and large, guilt manifests itself through repair-oriented activities, whereas shame manifests itself through escape- and withdrawal-oriented behaviors. These behavioral manifestations assist in explaining why guilt is often seen to be prosocial, whereas shame is generally considered antisocial. Regardless of whether one is experiencing guilt or shame, there are strategies for overcoming these emotions.

How to Conquer Guilt and Shame

As indicated by the desire to repair stated by guilty (and, to a lesser extent, shameful) persons, the greatest method to resolve feelings of shame or guilt is to correct the wrong that caused the guilt or shame.

This may entail just apologizing for a wrongdoing, replacing a broken item, or otherwise repairing the damage inflicted.

Even yet, one may experience guilt and humiliation following an apology, and it is critical to understand how to alleviate these feelings. This is frequently accomplished through self-forgiveness, particularly when the wrongdoer does not forgive the person who injured them.

Individuals prone to guilt are more likely to self-forgive, whereas individuals prone to shame are less likely. This is critical because self-forgiveness is a technique to transcend guilt and shame without ignoring the real harm one may have caused.

However, one hopeful study discovered that a self-directed workbook could assist individuals in forgiving themselves. This suggests that even shame-prone individuals who are less inclined to forgive themselves can take efforts toward forgiveness. The study's workbook is now freely available online. (Check out in attached sources file at the end of the book.)

Another study indicated that mindfulness was an effective strategy to lessen emotions of shame in patients with borderline personality disorder (BPD, an illness that is partially defined by persistent, high levels of shame). Participants who completed a ten-minute guided mindful breathing session experienced decreased feelings of shame.

Interestingly, this study also discovered that loving-kindness meditation (LKM) was ineffective at reducing shame when compared to a control condition, albeit the authors speculate that this could be because LKM "needs gradual cultivation." In either case, mindful breathing appears to be an accessible method of reducing shame.

Another strategy for alleviating feelings of shame is to convert them to thoughts of guilt. That is, rather than feeling horrible about themselves for the harm they have caused, one can feel bad about their acts and behaviors.

While some people are more prone to guilt and others to shame, this deliberate self-blame transference can occur. This can also be accomplished by recognizing that the harm one has caused repairable and that feelings of shame associated with that harm can be overcome.

Worksheets on Guilt and Shame – see online resources
You will find some helpful worksheets for individuals seeking actionable strategies for reducing feelings of guilt and shame or for individuals seeking strategies for confronting their feelings of guilt and shame.

Recognize and deal with guilt and shame
This worksheet defines guilt and then offers coping strategies. It then does the same thing with shame. Although this worksheet looks geared toward those who lead drug abuse support groups,

it might be beneficial for both individuals and those who have struggled with guilt and shame in the absence of substance usage.

Moving forward: six steps to self-forgiveness

Mindful breathing

Although this worksheet is not expressly about guilt or shame, mindful breathing has been demonstrated in the study to help alleviate emotions of shame. This worksheet will assist anyone, regardless of their degree of mindfulness expertise, begin a mindful breathing practice. YouTube videos may benefit individuals who prefer to follow along with guided sessions.

Finally, guilt and shame are critical social emotions because they prevent people from acting solely in their self-interest. While it is necessary to acknowledge and seek to repair the damage that has resulted in guilt and shame, it is also necessary to forgive oneself when a sincere endeavor has been made to repair the damage. Otherwise, feelings of guilt and shame can have detrimental effects.

Additionally, individuals must forgive those who have harmed them when the transgressor recognizes the harm they have caused and attempts to heal it.

While everyone has the right to self-protection and to request preparatory acts following wrongdoing, everyone also has the right to forgiveness once they have rectified the damage or made credible attempts to do so. After all, guilt and shame are fundamentally intended to contribute to developing a more compassionate and just society.

Guilt Game

GOOD FOR
ME
GOOD FOR
OTHERS
GUILT-FREE
SWEET
SPOT
GOOD FOR
THE PLANET

My-mindguide.com

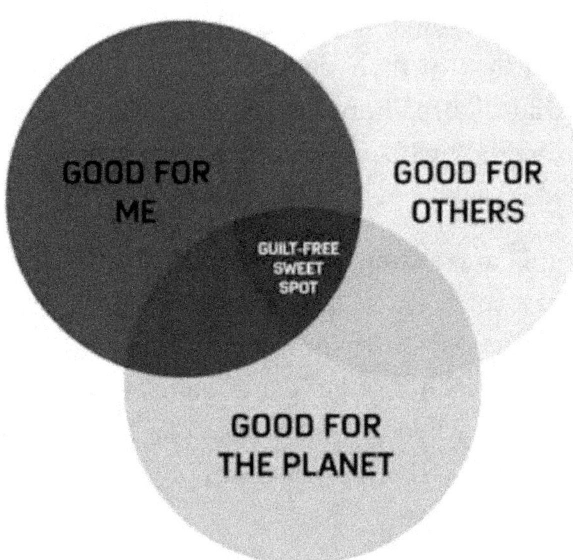

RECOVERY FROM GUILT AND SHAME

While the phrases 'guilt' and shame are frequently used interchangeably, they are not synonymous. Shame is defined as:

1) the unpleasant sensations evoked by the awareness of something dishonorable, indecent, or absurd done by oneself or another,
2) vulnerability to this emotion,
3) disgrace, and
4) a circumstance eliciting regret or disgrace.

Guilt is described as the following:
1) what it means to be guilty of doing something wrong or breaking the rules;
2) a sense of responsibility or remorse for some offence, real or imagined; and
3) conduct constituting the commission of such crimes or wrongs.

The major difference between shame and guilt is that when we feel ashamed, we think we're terrible; when we feel guilty, we think we've done something bad. Shame reflects who we are; guilt reflects our actions.

These two emotions contribute significantly to internal anguish and frequently prompt people to punish themselves, inflicting further misery. Individuals who deal with substance misuse frequently have deep-seated issues with guilt and shame, the majority of which arise from their youth when they had no choice in the matter. Using drugs and alcohol obscured these sensations and certainly resulted in further instances for which to feel guilty or ashamed. It can quickly spiral into a vicious cycle of self-abuse. Feeling guilty or chastised for previous offences does nothing to heal the body or mind or aid in our recovery. Nobody is without flaws. We have all done things we are not proud of at some point, whether we have an addiction. Dwelling on these emotions simply serves to hinder our lives' growth.

If guilt and shame are persistently plaguing your mind and impairing your happiness and well-being, there is hope. It takes deliberate effort to overcome these emotions.

Here are a few suggestions that work:
- Accept it - When feelings of guilt, remorse, or shame arise, do not attempt to flee or conceal them. Allow yourself to experience these emotions. Take ownership of things, experience them, and then go on. You cannot alter history.

- Correct it – When we are addicted, we may do things that we would not have otherwise done. If you have taken acts that have harmed people you care about, attempt to rectify the situation. For instance, if you stole money, make restitution. If you've broken trust, keeping clean and sober one day at a time is an effective method to reclaim it from the people you care about.

- Apologize - Expressing regret for wrongs committed can go a long way. Being sorry implies that we will do everything possible to avoid committing that wrong again.

- Forgive yourself - It is critical to forgive ourselves. Guilt and shame have a detrimental effect on our self-esteem. Forgive yourself and make a concerted effort to avoid repeating your errors.

- Surround yourself with positive people - Establish a network of positive people. Take a break from those who are continually criticizing you for your mistakes. All persons in recovery must learn their boundaries and what is healthy. We may not completely distance ourselves from some people, but we can stand our position, make amends, and request that they refrain from bringing up the past.

- Write - Writing serves as a cathartic outlet. You may write about incidents that caused you to feel guilty or ashamed. This is analogous to performing the fourth step. Digging deep to discover the source of these emotions enables us to recognize and heal from them. A lined notepad and a pen or pencil are required.

1. Make a list of everything you believe you've done incorrectly, beginning with the most recent event and going backwards in time. After each entry, leave six lines.

2. Justify your actions under each entry.

3. Indicate in the third line which was harmed by this conduct.

4. In the fourth line, describe how you might have done things differently.

5. In the fifth line, describe what you can do to rectify the situation.

Once you've jotted everything down, you'll be prepared to move forward with the solutions you wrote. Confronting our emotions and learning to manage and overcome them helps boost the recovery process and prevent a recurrence.

MAKING PEACE WITH GUILT: REMOVING HARM

Consider guilt to be feeling awful about something you did that was wrong or hurtful, or, more precisely, the sensation of disgust associated with negative thinking. Thus, existential shame is a fictitious sensation or emotion. Shame is defined as the belief that you are a lousy, awful, or nasty person, accompanied by a sense of disgust and a negative mental assessment.

Existential guilt responds to actual harm, such as physical, cognitive, emotional, or interpersonal injury. Effectively resolving and making peace with guilt is critical for healthy development. Here are two critical elements that serve as a straightforward litmus test for existential guilt: (1) demonstrate why this activity is wrong, such as murder, and (2) demonstrate the real harm committed, such as an injury or violation. In my view, not much qualifies as ethically wrong, even in the extreme case of murder, and not much qualifies as actual harm. If you are aware of either, you are experiencing existential guilt. Generally, whatever occurred does not constitute existential guilt. Rather than that, it is 'imagined guilt,' in which you believe you have done something wrong but have not. You never looked to verify. Pausing to check for oneself is critical in avoiding carrying something that is not yours.

For most people, one estimate is that of all the guilt they carry and continue to accumulate, possibly 10% at the most and less than 1% at the very least counts as guilt for wrongdoing or direct injury. The remainder is imagined guilt, which is worth acknowledging, releasing, and regaining a sense of self-worth. In such situations, you can take pleasure in boldly saying, "Cancel and erase," numerous times and instantly replace it with a self-validating phrase, such as "I know I did not harm, I'm a good person, and I can make a difference." In such situations, every one of us can realistically breathe a sigh of relief.

What are your options if, after checking with reality, you or someone else is found to have committed an act of wrongdoing and causing harm, for which you now suffer existential guilt? A straightforward method to resolving guilt and completing the experience can be extremely beneficial in terms of reestablishing harmony with yourself and clearing the air, and reestablishing harmony in your relationship. This assists in the healing of wounds to one's integrity and relationships. Three critical steps are as follows:

- To begin, express your responsibility to the harmed individual or individuals; state, "I did this." This is an excellent opportunity to linger, look the other person directly in the eye, honestly state what you did and simply own it.

- Second, give your unequivocal commitment and word of honor to refrain from repeating this harmful act and to take only good, responsible actions going forward; state, "I commit and give you my word that this harm will not occur again; instead, I promise to take only these good, responsible actions going forward."

- Ask verbally what you need to do to repair the harm and put things right again; for example, "I want to make this right with you; what can I do now to put this behind us completely?" Often, simply stating your possessions suffices. If there was some material loss, this loss might be requested to bring the harmful episode to a close and put you both behind bars. Occasionally, it may be appropriate to help the wounded individual or community somehow.

Certain individuals with a religious or moral background may wish for those who caused harm to express their regret for their actions. They may believe an apology and a request for forgiveness are also important. The following two steps are advantageous in this instance:

- You can express your regret for what you did and the hurt you caused; state, "I'm remorseful for what I did. I now understand the harm that resulted from it, and I regret it."

- Apologize verbally and seek forgiveness for your actions. Be VERY SPECIFIC about the subject. "I apologize and beg your pardon for..."

After all of this has been communicated honestly, the person who committed the harm can inquire whether the affected person is satisfied, and the situation is concluded. This is frequently the case. Unfortunately, some people are good at harboring grudges and will never let go of the occurrence. Thankfully, this is a rather infrequent occurrence in my experience. When this occurs, it is appropriate to advise the grudge holder that the situation has concluded for you. If they persist in carrying it, it is a truly bad scenario; this excruciating load is totally their own, and you wash your hands of it.

As long as the hazardous conduct, including addictive behaviors, is not reenacted, bringing it up is 'off-limits,' even in the heat of an argument. When one has kept their word in action, and the other party wishes to bring up an old issue that has not resurfaced, this is referred to as "playing low ball" and reflects poorly on the perpetrator. Indeed, it is now their responsibility to clean up this mess! Of course, it's reasonable to weigh the history of the injuring party's bad behavior when they restart the hurtful action. To prevent harming others, some believe it's better to die telling the truth than ever to admit wrongdoing. Occasionally, as with past affairs, nothing positive may come from speaking out today, even more so if this behavior has ceased because of your honest growth and maturation. Proper judgment requires weighing the potential harm to the injured party caused by your admission against the harm caused by not owning and cleaning up the situation with them. Now, find tranquility.

Guilt Game

My-mindguide.com

IN PHILOSOPHY, THE CONCEPTS OF GUILT AND SHAME

PHILOSOPHY OF GUILT

Guilt is a widely misunderstood emotion that has long endured an unjustified, negative reputation. The popular press is replete with pieces offering advice on how to live a guilt-free life, many therapists recognize guilt reduction as a short-term therapy objective, and no one wants to be labelled a guilt-inducing mother. However, much of the stigma attached to guilt can be traced to people's penchant for conflating guilt with shame. As it turns out, current research indicates that guilt is the more adaptive emotion on balance, strengthening relationships in various ways while avoiding the numerous hidden costs associated with shame.

Guilt has been defined differently as a moral, self-conscious, social, and problematic feeling, highlighting the complexities of this affective experience and guilt's numerous roles in people's lives. At the very least, systematic theoretical analyses of guilt date back to Sigmund Freud, who considered guilt to be a reaction to superego norms violations. According to Freud, guilt occurs when inappropriate ego-directed activities or id-driven urges clash with the superego's moral demands. Freud regarded guilt as a normal aspect of the human experience. However, he saw unresolved or suppressed guilt as a critical component of many psychological illnesses. Throughout the decades, guilt was mostly confined to psychoanalytic theory. Until the mid-1960s, little scientific research on guilt was undertaken, and few psychological researchers distinguished between shame and guilt until the late 1980s affected the revolution.

How Are Guilt and Shame Differ?

The phrases guilt and shame are frequently used interchangeably, either as moral feelings that restrict socially inappropriate behavior or as troublesome emotions that contribute significantly to various psychological disorders. An increasing body of recent research, on the other hand, argues that these are distinct emotional states. Guilt and shame are self-blaming feelings that can respond to many failures, indiscretions, and social blunders. The critical distinction between these two emotions is in the direction of one's negative opinion. When individuals experience guilt, they feel awful about a particular behavior—about something they have done. When people experience shame, they feel inferior to others. This distinction between self ("I did that dreadful thing") and conduct ("I did that horrible thing") has a significant impact on both the emotion's experience and its consequences for psychological adjustment and interpersonal behavior. Whereas feelings of shame (about oneself) contain a sense of shrinking, worthlessness, and a desire to flee the shame-inducing setting, feelings of guilt (about a specific behavior) involve a sense of tension, remorse, and regret. Individuals experiencing guilt frequently report nagging attention or preoccupation with the offence, replaying it in their minds and wishing they had behaved differently. Rather than inspiring a desire to conceal, guilt frequently stimulates reparative behavior: confessing, apologizing, or correcting the harm done. Thus, guilt is more likely to keep people engaged constructively in a guilt-inducing circumstance.

A benefit of guilt is that the scope of responsibility is less expansive and far-reaching than that of shame. In guilt, one's primary preoccupation is with a specific behavior that is somewhat independently of the self. Because guilt does not jeopardize one's fundamental identity, it is less likely to prompt protective denial or reaction than shame. In practice, guilt presents a far more controllable challenge than shame does. It is significantly easier to modify negative conduct than change a negative self.

The Moral Emotion of Guilt Appears to Be the More Adaptive

Five sets of research findings indicate that guilt, in comparison to shame, is the more moral and adaptive emotion. To begin, shame and guilt result in opposed drives or behavior patterns. Normally, shame is related to wanting to deny, conceal, or escape; typically, guilt is associated with a wish to rectify. In this way, guilt tends to steer individuals in a constructive, proactive, and forward-looking path, whereas shame tends to steer people toward separation, distancing, and defense.

Second, it appears as though there is a unique connection between guilt and empathy. Understanding another person's perspective and empathizing with their feelings are two of the most important aspects of interpersonal empathy. Empathy, in turn, encourages prosocial, helpful action, suppresses aggression and is a necessary component of warm, satisfying partnerships. Numerous studies of children, adolescents, and adults demonstrate that prone to guilt individuals are generally empathic. (By contrast, shame-proneness relates to a decreased ability for other-directed empathy and a tendency toward self-directed personal distress responses.) Similar findings arise when addressing present-moment sensations of shame and guilt. According to a study published in the Journal of Personality and Social Psychology, guilt and shame are two distinct emotions. Yet, both can be characterized by empathy and concern for the victims of their actions. By focusing on poor behavior (rather than a terrible self), those experiencing guilt avoid the egocentric, self-involved process of shame. Rather than that, their emphasis on that particular conduct draws attention to the implications of that behavior for disturbed individuals, eliciting an empathic response.

Thirdly, maybe due to the link between guilt and empathy, guilt-prone individuals are more likely to manage and express their anger constructively. While guilt-prone individuals are about as likely as the average person to feel angry in daily life, once irritated, they are more likely to work toward resolving the issue in an open, nonhostile manner, utilizing their anger to effect positive change. For example, when people feel angry, they are motivated to resolve the situation, are less likely to act aggressive, and are more inclined to debate the issue openly and logically. By contrast, those prone to feelings of shame (about the full self) are more likely to express their anger through aggressive and other damaging behaviors.

Fourth, research indicates that guilt is beneficial in assisting people in avoiding sin and remaining on a moral path throughout life. For instance, guilt-proneness relates to statements such as "I would not steal something I needed, even if I were certain I could get away with it." Adolescents who experience shame are less likely to become delinquent than their guilt-free classmates. Children who experience shame-free guilt in fifth grade are less likely to be arrested, convicted, and jailed as young adults. They are more likely to engage in safe sex and are less likely to engage in substance misuse. In a longitudinal study of incarcerated inmates, guilt-proneness was associated with decreased rates of recidivism and substance misuse in the first year following release.

Finally, contrary to popular opinion, guilt-free behavior does not entail significant psychological adjustment and well-being costs. When measures that account for the distinction between shame (about oneself) and guilt (about a specific behavior) are applied, the propensity to experience guilt is found to be mostly unrelated to psychiatric symptoms. Numerous independent studies agree on one thing: shame, but not guilt, is associated with anxiety, sadness, low self-esteem, and a variety of other psychiatric difficulties.

When Does Guilt Become Maladaptive?

Why is guilt usually cited as a symptom of anxiety and depression? What is this chronic, ruminative guilt that so many therapists talk about? One explanation is that many of these troubling guilt experiences combine guilt and shame. It appears likely that when a person begins with a guilt experience ("Oh, what an awful thing I've done") but then magnifies and generalizes the event to the self ("...and am I not a horrible person"), many of the benefits of guilt are lost. Not only is a person confronted with stress and sorrow over an unresolved behavior, but they are also burdened with sentiments of contempt and hatred for a poor, imperfect self. Guilt that has been infused with shame may be just as troublesome as shame itself.

It is essential to note that most measures used to distinguish shame from guilt focus on situations where responsibility or blame is clearly established. Individuals are tasked with imagining instances in which they blatantly failed or committed a transgression. Problems are likely to ensue when people develop an inflated or misguided sense of responsibility for situations beyond their control. Survivor guilt is a classic example of this type of troubling emotional reaction, which has constantly been related to post-traumatic stress disorder and other psychological disorders.

Is Guilt Beneficial?
The benefits of guilt are most visible when individuals recognize their failings and trespasses and accept appropriate responsibility. In such circumstances, it appears as though the interpersonal benefits of guilt do not come at an unreasonable cost. The propensity for shame-free guilt in reaction to obvious infractions is largely unrelated to psychiatric issues, but shame is regularly associated with maladaptive processes and outcomes on several levels. When it comes to the individual's welfare, the welfare of their relationships, and the welfare of society, guilt is the moral emotion of choice.

PHILOSOPHY OF SHAME

Shame Definition

Shame is one of the most underappreciated emotions among Western countries. While shame can dramatically influence one's psychological adjustment and interpersonal interactions, these feelings frequently go unnoticed. Individuals rarely discuss their experiences with shame. Denial and a need for concealment are intrinsic to the shame phenomenology. Individuals withdraw from their feelings of shame, just as they withdraw from others during a shame encounter. To add to the confusion, shame can masquerade as other emotions, hiding behind guilt or rage, fueling despair and sadness.

The tendency for people to conflate shame with guilt contributed to shame being relegated to a footnote in the first century of psychology. In professional literature and common discourse, shame and guilt are frequently used interchangeably as emotion synonyms, or (possibly more frequently), guilt is employed as a catch-all term for both emotions' components. Even Sigmund Freud, the father of psychoanalysis, rarely distinguished between shame and guilt.

The Distinction Between Shame and Guilt

Numerous psychologists and anthropologists have made efforts to disentangle these moral sentiments. Three types of accounts of the distinction between shame and guilt exist:

1. A distinction between the types of events that evoke emotions.

2. A differentiation between the public versus the private character of the transgression.

3. There is a distinction between the degree to which the individual regards the emotion-eliciting event as a failing of self or behavior.

Theorists who focus on specific occurrences assume that certain situations result in shame, while others result in guilt. For instance, activities that injure others elicit guilt, but behaviors that break social rules generate shame (e.g., burping in public, poor table manners, atypical sexual conduct). However, social psychological research reveals that the occurrence has an unexpectedly small effect on the distinction between shame and guilt. When people are asked to recount their shame and guilt experiences, most occurrences (e.g., lying, cheating, stealing, sex, failing to aid another, defying parents) are associated with feelings of shame for some and guilt for others. It has been suggested that whereas guilt has traditionally related to moral breaches (e.g. injuring others or disobeying societal norms), shame may be more broadly related to a wider range of situations, encompassing moral and nonmoral failures and transgressions. However, the situations that result in shame and guilt are strikingly similar.

Another widely mentioned distinction between shame and guilt is the long-held belief that shame is a more public emotion, resulting from public exposure and rejection. In contrast, guilt is a more private sensation. As it turns out, research does not support this in terms of the situation's actual features. People's admissions about their shame and guilt experiences reveal that others are no more likely to be aware of shame-inducing actions than they are of guilt-inducing acts.

Where did the concept of shame as a more public feeling originate? Although both shame and guilt-inducing situations are similarly public (in the possibility that others are present and aware of the failure or violation), when people feel shame, they pay attention to different factors than when they feel guilt. When individuals experience responsibility, they are bound to know about their effect on others (e.g., how much an imprudent comment hurt a companion or the amount they frustrated their folks). In the examination, when individuals experience disgrace, they are more worried about how others will see them (e.g., whether a companion could think the person is a jerk or whether the guardians could see the person in question as a disappointment). In short, when people experience shame, they frequently focus on the opinions of others, but actual public exposure is no more likely than when they experience guilt.

A third contrast between shame and guilt is based on the object of one's unfavorable assessment, and this is the one that social psychology research most strongly supports. When individuals experience guilt, they feel awful about certain behavior. When people experience shame, they feel inferior to others. Although this distinction between self ("I did that dreadful thing") and activity ("I did that horrible thing") may appear slight, it lays the groundwork for profoundly divergent emotional experiences, motivational patterns, and subsequent conduct.

Shame is a particularly terrible feeling since it involves one's basic self, not only one's behavior. Shame is an agonizing examination of one's full self, the conviction that "I am an inadequate, incompetent, or nasty person." Individuals experiencing shame frequently report a sense of shrinking, of being little. They believe they are useless and weak. Additionally, they feel exposed. Although shame may not always require an actual audience witnessing one's flaws, it frequently involves a vision of how one's damaged self might appear to others—as unworthy and repulsive.

Shame-Related Motivations and Behaviors

According to empirical research, shame frequently promotes avoidance, defensiveness, and denial. Individuals experiencing shame frequently express a desire to flee the situation, to "sink into the floor and vanish." It is not commonplace for individuals to deny responsibility for their actions (or the behavior itself). Individuals who are shamed are inclined to conceal their transgressions and their very selves from others to avoid the anguish of shame. Along with encouraging avoidant conduct, research shows that shame frequently results in the externalization of blame and wrath. Initially, animosity toward the self is aimed during a shame experience ("I'm such a loser"). However, because this requires such a comprehensive negative self-assessment, the individual experiencing shame is likely to feel trapped and overwhelmed. As a result, embarrassed individuals tend to become defensive. One strategy for self-protection and regaining control is to turn that hate and blame outward. Rather than taking responsibility for hurting a friend's feelings, for example, ashamed people are more likely to make excuses, deny saying anything objectionable, and even blame the friend for overreacting or misinterpreting them. Not all anger is motivated by shame; nonetheless, irrational rage and anger that appear to come out of nowhere are motivated by underlying feelings of shame.

In extreme cases, shame can manifest through hostility and violence, with tragic results. Clinicians and researchers have identified shame as a typical component in domestic abuse scenarios. In the months preceding the Columbine massacre and previous school shootings, the shooters appear to have struggled with intense emotions of humiliation. Collective shame and humiliation have been recognized as a cause of the ethnic struggle, genocide, and international conflict by historians and political analysts.

Embarrassment and Psychiatric Symptoms

Researchers frequently indicate a link between shame and various psychological symptoms, including depression, anxiety, PTSD, substance addiction, eating disorders, sexual dysfunction, and suicidal ideation. Individuals who frequently experience shame are more likely to acquire psychological symptoms than their peers who do not experience shame.

Is Shame a Moral Emotion at All?

Shame is frequently said to be a moral emotion resulting from significant moral or social standards transgressions. A widely held concept is that people avoid transgression and impropriety by avoiding shameful thoughts and feelings. Surprisingly little research suggests that shame is a deterrent. Shame is not as efficient as guilt at directing one's behavior morally. Adults' self-reported moral activities, for example, are significantly positively linked with a penchant for guilt but not with a propensity for shame.

Similarly, youngsters who have a developed capacity for guilt are less likely to be arrested and imprisoned throughout their adolescent years. Children who are prone to embarrassment are not as fortunate. Guilt, but not shame, is connected with lower "criminal thinking" in jailed criminals. With research tying shame to diminished empathy, denial of responsibility, and damaging outbursts of fury, there is cause to doubt shame's moral self-regulation function.

Shame's Adaptive Functions

Thus far, the theory and research have stressed the negative aspects of shame, emphasizing its detrimental effects on psychological adjustment and interpersonal behavior. Why, therefore, are people capable of experiencing this emotion? What adaptive function could it possibly serve?"

Psychologists using a sociobiological lens have concentrated on the appealing functions of shame. It is a critical indicator to dominant apes that lower-ranked animals acknowledge their place in the social order of apes. Submissive, shame-like emotions (hunched posture, downcast gaze) reinforce the social order and appear to dissipate violent confrontations. When subordinates show surrender in this manner, dominant apes are significantly less inclined to attack. Most likely, shame had a comparable purpose at earlier phases of human evolution. Additionally, it has been proposed that the impulse to withdraw, which is frequently associated with shame, may be beneficial in interrupting potentially dangerous social encounters until the shamed individual can regroup. In general, the weight of scientific evidence indicates that guilt is the more moral, adaptive response to crimes and violations in a modern human community that is more egalitarian in form than hierarchical.

Guilt Game

My-mindguide.com

MANAGING GUILT OBTAINING POSITIVE RESULTS FROM NEGATIVE EMOTIONS

Are you resentful about something?
Perhaps you made an unflattering remark about one of your teammates. Or perhaps you're divided between the demands of work life and home life, fearful of devoting insufficient time or attention to either.

Regardless of the circumstance, guilt can be an unbearable burden to carry. If left unchecked, it can nibble away at you and drag you down. You may even avoid others to conceal your guilt or behave impulsively as a result of your emotions.

However, guilt can be a highly beneficial emotion. The study indicates that, at its most helpful, it serves as a reminder that you can improve in the future. Experiencing it also demonstrates that you possess moral and ethical principles and empathy.

Occasionally, however, we experience unreasonable guilt for events outside of our control. If left unchecked, this can be detrimental. This section discusses the various types of guilt and how to deal with them.

Why Am I Guilty?

Guilt is the sensation we experience when we let ourselves or others down by not meeting a certain standard. This standard may be universally recognized (missing a deadline and delaying a project, say). It can also be self-imposed: a self-perceived failure to live up to one's values.

There are two types of guilt in general: "good" and "unhealthy." It's critical to know the type of shame you're experiencing whenever you do. A short time later, you'll be in a superior situation to manage it.

If you're feeling guilty, it's critical to distinguish between "good" and "unhealthy" behaviors.

Recognizing Healthy Guilt

Healthy guilt is reasonable or fair. It's the terrible emotion you have when you realize you've behaved inappropriately.

When you injure someone or cause a problem that you could have otherwise been avoided, you will experience healthy guilt. Guilt informs you that you need to make amends and alter your behavior.

Experiencing Unhealthy Guilt

Unhealthy guilt is excessive, ill-placed, and unreasonable. This is when you feel terrible about something but are not responsible for it or have no control over the circumstance.

Consider a friend experiencing a significant career setback while you receive a promotion. Despite your satisfaction with your accomplishments, you feel sorry for them and guilty about your happiness. This guilt is irrational and unhealthy, as you do not influence the circumstances that led to it. It serves no one – and you have committed no wrong!

"Survivor guilt" is an extreme example. For instance, due to the unexpected loss of jobs caused by COVID-19, some persons who remain employed may experience survivor guilt.

Pathological guilt is difficult to treat because there isn't much that can be done to make things better. Instead, the goal is to improve your reasoning abilities.

How to Handle Healthy Guilt

It can be terrible to feel guilty about doing something wrong. When it does occur, though, you can use it to strengthen your relationships and drive personal growth.

Consider the following methods for coping with good guilt:

Acknowledge and Apologize

If your guilt impacts another individual, apologize immediately and make your apologies unconditional. Do not attempt to excuse your conduct or to place blame on others, even if they were involved. Simply acknowledge your anger, annoyance, or pain.

Simply bringing the issue to light in this manner can help significantly in resolving the situation. You might even discover that the individual is already "over it." However, even if the person you've offended does not immediately accept your apology, you've acknowledged and accepted responsibility for your conduct.

Make Modifications Quickly

Find a solution to rectify the situation, and do so immediately. Delaying this step and letting even legitimate feelings of guilt accumulate might cause you anxiety and does nothing to alleviate the other person's sorrow.

Make your acts beneficial. For instance, if you overlook something critical and burden a colleague with more work, volunteer to inform their management that you were to blame. Then assist in the work. This will be more beneficial than inviting them to lunch.

Modification of Your Behavior

Your guilty behavior may be a one-time occurrence, such as saying something insensitive. Alternatively, it could be something you do often, such as poor record-keeping, that generates recurring problems for your coworkers.

It is critical to take the lead and address the problematic conduct. This could include honing your time management and delegating abilities to establish a more balanced work-life and overcome negative habits.

Positive improvements will enhance your interactions with others and help you avoid frequent feelings of guilt. Consider approaching your boss for assistance with desired habits, as they may provide training or advice.

Accept and Proceed

If you've done everything possible to make amends and prevent a recurrence of the circumstance, let go of the guilt. The sooner you overcome it, the sooner you can turn your attention to more productive activities. Accepting your sentiments and initiating the process of self-forgiveness can be beneficial with mindfulness.

Additionally, you can use your experiences to cultivate Emotional Intelligence. This can assist you in comprehending and regulating your own emotions, allowing you to handle your guilt effectively.

Tip:

If you're having difficulty moving on, utilize the same technique you would with a friend. You're likely to accept their apologies and move on if they apologize. Treat yourself with the same decency - otherwise, you risk succumbing to unhealthy guilt.

How to Deal with Irresponsible Guilt

Unhealthy guilt provides none of the benefits associated with healthy guilt, and it can be difficult to overcome. However, managing your emotions and maintaining a more balanced perspective with the appropriate tactics is possible.

Maintain a Balanced View on What You Can Control

Begin by noting the factors that you can truly control in a circumstance. Afterward, write down all the things you can't do. Take responsibility for your actions, and do not let anyone else's words or deeds cloud your judgment. The longer your second list, the more likely your guilt is unfounded and ill-advised.

Don't worry about things you can't change. Make an effort to affect only those components of the situation under your control. And, where necessary, develop a plan to address them.

It is acceptable to acknowledge your "survival" fortunate and empathize with others. However, you should recognize that feeling bad about it can be taxing. Attempting to snap out of it and move on, on the other hand, is being dishonest about your sentiments.

Rather than that, use the power of guilt-related emotions to motivate you to take constructive action. This will instill a sense of control in an otherwise powerless situation. Our essay on the Control Influence Accept Model may assist this situation.

For instance, you can assist someone by not avoiding them out of embarrassment or by taking the time to listen and acknowledge their circumstance. Simply inquiring about someone's wants or needs can make a difference.

Whether or not you assist others, you can also choose to "seize the day" and make the most of your "fortune" - by performing at your best. Purpose in the aftermath of a traumatic event transforms survivor remorse into gratitude and action.

Make Use of Affirmations

You can overcome persistent or recurring unreasonable emotions of guilt by suppressing negative self-talk and soliciting the opinions of others for a more objective perspective. Then, using affirmations, reinforce the message that the circumstance is not your fault.

After establishing the aspects of the circumstance over which you have control and those over which you have no control, address them with a simple positive statement. For instance, "I was promoted ahead of Kyle because I possessed a superior combination of talents and experience," rather than "I was promoted ahead of Kyle even though he has been here longer. Thus I must have been pushy and over-ambitious."

Tip:

An effective affirmation for various circumstances is "I did the best I could with the information I had."

Confront Perfectionism

You may feel guilty due to your overly high standards for yourself. This can result in guilt for things you haven't done or haven't done well enough, even if they aren't your fault. Simultaneously, you completely overlook your accomplishments.

Take time to think on and challenge your perfectionist tendencies to refocus your standards. Additionally, keep in mind that nobody is flawless!

Be Assertive

You're likely feeling guilty about a scenario because someone else is oblivious to the unrealistic expectations they're applying to you.

Alternatively, someone may be purposefully influencing you to induce guilt to control your actions. Certain individuals are exceptionally adept at identifying and capitalizing on their coworkers' feelings of guilt.

Consider the manager who constantly requests that team members work long hours "for the greater welfare of the team" – and indirectly implies that anyone wanting a healthy work-life balance should do the same. is "an individual who is not a team player." This may elicit guilt for no apparent cause.

In these cases, stand up for yourself and, if you are clear that you are not in the wrong, deliver your message firmly and assertively.

Warning: Negative thinking linked with pathological guilt can be a symptom of depression, burnout, or OCD and result in serious health problems.

The approaches described in this section may have a beneficial effect on lowering unhealthy guilt, but they are provided for informational purposes only. Always seek professional help if you have concerns about connected illnesses or if continual feelings of guilt are causing considerable or chronic unhappiness.

Guilt creates stress and impairs performance at work. The absence of intervention can seriously harm relationships and contribute to mental health issues.

There are two distinct categories of guilt. Healthy guilt entails acknowledging your wrongdoing and utilizing it to motivate you to better your relationships and behavior by:

- Apologizing.
- Apologizing.
- Modifying one's behavior.
- Acknowledging your shortcomings and moving on.

This is unhealthy guilt when you feel sorry about fictitious or beyond your control. While shifting can be difficult, you can manage your emotions by:

- Recognize what you can and cannot control.
- Putting your standards to the test.
- Affirming the situation's favorable elements.
- Being forceful with those who attempt to guilt you.

SEVEN WAYS TO AVOID GUILT TRIPS WITHOUT INJURING ANYONE

Guilt trips have a cost that both parties should avoid.

Guilt trips are verbal or nonverbal communication in which the guilt inducer attempts to instill guilt in the target to exert control over their conduct. As such, guilt trips constitute blatant psychological manipulation and coercion.

However, guilt trips are rarely spoken of in such harsh terms. Rather than that, we perceive them as things mothers say to coax their children into eating another bowl of soup ("I slaved over a stove for three hours for you to have only one matzo ball?") or as something fathers do to coax their children into conforming ("Fine, don't attend your niece's confirmation. I suppose your family and beliefs are no longer important to you.").

Why Guilt Trips Are Frequently Successful

While guilt trips are a staple of many families' interactions, they are rarely as benign as we believe. While they frequently "succeed" because the recipient's behavior changes. As a result, these "successes" always come at a cost—one that few guilt inducers consider: Guilt trips typically produce intense feelings of remorse and intense feelings of hatred toward the manipulator.

The typical nature of the connections between the two people enables guilt trips to succeed despite the hatred they generate. Guilt trips are most common in close family relationships (or close friendships) because if the target does not have strong feelings of caring and affection for the guilt inducer, their resentment and anger at being manipulated will likely outweigh their guilty feelings, causing them to resist the manipulation.

How Guilt Trips Poison Our Most Intimate Relationships

When those who induced guilt trips were asked to identify the possible repercussions of their actions, only 2% indicated animosity. In other words, individuals who engage in guilt trips are typically wholly focused on achieving their desired outcome and are completely unaware of the potential harm their actions may create. As mild as the poisonous consequences of most guilt trips, their toxicity can accumulate over time, causing substantial stresses and emotional estrangement. Ironically, the most prevalent motif of familial guilt trips is interpersonal neglect, suggesting that guilt trips' long-term effect is likely to be the polar opposite of what most guilt trippers desire.

Seven Techniques for Limiting Guilt Trippers

The most effective strategy to mitigate the harm that guilt trips do to our relationships is to establish boundaries with the guilt inducer and encourage them to change their habits. This is how:

1. Reassure the individual that you understand how important it is for them that you do what they're attempting to shame you into doing.

2. Explain that their use of guilt to coerce you into complying with their wishes makes you feel angry, even if you ultimately comply.

3. Express your fear that accumulating this kind of resentments may cause you to feel further distanced from them, which neither you nor they desire.

4. Request that they communicate their wishes directly, to take ownership of the request rather than attempting to engage your conscience, and to respect your decisions when you make them (e.g., "I'd love to have another bowl of soup. No?

A brisket is provided for you, or "It would mean a great deal to me if you could attend your niece's confirmation, but I understand if your schedule does not permit it."

5. Explain that you will frequently comply with their requests if they are more direct. Acknowledge that you may not always comply with their demands, but emphasize the payoff—that when you choose to respond positively, you will do it truly, feel good about it, and gain even more.

6. Be prepared to have reminder discussions and contact them regarding future guilt trips (and they will). Adapting to a new way of communicating will take time.

7. Maintain a spirit of kindness and patience throughout this process. This will drive them to change more than if you approach them with wrath and hate, however justified your feelings may be.

SIX TECHNIQUES FOR OVERCOMING DAILY GUILT

For many of us, shame is like an old friend—someone we willingly let in and can't get out.

Guilt manifests itself when our actions contradict our aims and values—whether we procrastinate, breach a commitment, or take credit for someone else's effort. At its best, guilt functions as a moral compass, forcing us to reflect on our actions (or lack thereof) and then effect positive change.

However, we find ourselves cohabiting with a parasite when guilt establishes a long-term presence, dishing out regular servings of blame and shame without providing anything useful. Guilt casts a pall over the positive aspects of our existence. It depletes our energy and self-esteem. That is when we begin depriving ourselves of our particular desires and wants. We develop a pattern of placing ourselves last, feeding our guilt, and starving our self-esteem, making it increasingly difficult to be our fullest, brightest, and most creative selves.

Here are five telltale symptoms that guilt is eroding your life's quality:

- You avoid certain persons or situations out of embarrassment.
- You decline opportunities because you believe you do not deserve them.
- You withdraw or become defensive.
- Even when no one is challenging you, you rationalize or make excuses.
- When you relive the criminal deed in your thoughts, it depletes your mood and energy – and takes a long time to recover.

Three typical types of guilt can prevent us from living fully—if we allow them to. Rather than continuously kicking ourselves, let us instead kick out the guilt. The following are a couple of thoughts to kick you off.

The Guilt-Pleasure Conundrum

The term "guilt-free" is frequently used: guilt-free television, guilt-free desserts, guilt-free shopping. Whenever there is pleasure involved, there is an opportunity for guilt. We frequently deny ourselves what we desire because we assume we have not earned it. With the added pressure of feeling bad about saying yes, simple pleasures like a nightcap after work or a trip to the beach with friends become less pleasurable experiences.

Ironically, research indicates that guilt is a fairly ineffective method of behavior control. In a study published in Appetite in 2013, psychologists found that people who connected chocolate cake with guilt rather than happiness had a harder time losing and maintaining weight Rather than serving as a positive motivator, guilt fosters feelings of helplessness and lack of control.

While having guidelines for appropriate conduct is beneficial—a glass of wine with dinner is one thing; a bottle of wine is quite another—unrealistic expectations of never indulging set you up for failure. And a dreary existence.

Consider the following suggestions:

- **Relinquish Borrowed Beliefs**

If you believe that what you desire to accomplish is unjustified, consider who said that. Is society adamant that this is wrong? Your mother? Your elementary school baseball coach? Then inquire as to your own beliefs—and respect your judgment.

- **Calculate the Consequences**

What are the consequences of indulging? What steps would you be able to take to improve things? For instance, how can you compensate for the fact that is ordering dessert results in you slipping off your diet wagon? Perhaps a morning excursion to the gym? (Although you should probably avoid making this a habit.)

The Trap of a Guilty Conscience

A guilty conscience can serve as your own Alcatraz—rocky, labyrinthine, and impenetrable. However, punishing yourself by thinking about what a terrible person you are does not help you make up for the bad (or perhaps not-so-terrible) thing you did. Rather than that, it makes you self-absorbed and defensive. You cease putting your best foot forward, deceiving yourself and everyone around you.

The thing is, guilt without behavioral modification is a sham. If you have done something wrong—even if the victim is only yourself—acknowledge it, make an attempt to heal the damage, and resolve never to do it again. Once you are liberated from your guilty slammer, your world will become brighter and more brimming with possibilities.

Consider the following suggestions:

- **Self-Forgiveness**

Okay, so you committed an act of which you are not proud. That is a characteristic of humanity, but it does not define you. Self-forgiveness necessitates new perspectives. Discussing your remorse with another person frequently alleviates the stress. Much of the sting is usually removed when you express your thoughts aloud, but this may not occur in a single conversation. Additionally, you may try speaking to yourself as if you were another person. What would you say to another person in your situation?

- **Break Free From Your Guilt**

Once you've made genuine attempts to make amends, put your guilt in a box and dispose of it. Create a ritual that assists you in separating from your guilt—for example, write a positive affirmation or letter to yourself, or burn or discard a tangible relic that embodies your feelings of shame.

The Guilt-Inducing Perfection Myth

The bogeyman of perfection haunts us throughout our lives, and guilt (perfection's enfant terrible) rears its ugly head whenever we fall short of what we believe we should be — whether it's the woman who "has it all" or the straight-laced man.

A student who is fixated on achieving the greatest possible grade.

Often, this guilt is created by dread of disappointing others: you're a lousy parent because you missed a school play; you're a bad friend because you forgot a birthday; you don't deserve to be happy because your conservative family believes. You make poor choices.

Each time you fall short of the unattainable, you become more self-critical.

To alleviate the hate, attempt to refocus your mind on what is genuinely possible and devise tactical strategies for juggling and prioritizing life's numerous demands. Because when guilt takes over, and you attempt to please everyone, you end up pleasing no one—particularly yourself.

Consider the following suggestions:

- Activate the Peanut Gallery's mute function. When you're overcome with guilt for not being able to complete everything exactly, switch to a positive voice; for example, instead of "I served dinner 15 minutes late," switch to "I spent extra time perfecting the sauce, which I'm sure my friends will love."

- Accept Responsibility for Your Failures. Utilize this Failure Analysis Checklist to reflect on what went wrong and unearth critical insights that will assist you in preventing a recurrence of the circumstance. Our mistakes can help us grow in wisdom, intelligence, and compassion—but only if we stop wallowing in shame and embrace positive change.

FORGIVE YOURSELF FOR TAKING CARE OF YOURSELF WITHOUT FEELING GUILTY

How frequently do you feel guilty about self-care? Self-care guilt manifests in a variety of ways: apologizing for spending time for yourself, feeling self-indulgent, or deferring it in favor of more productive tasks.

Regardless of the reason, there is a nagging voice in your mind that makes you feel bad for self-care (even selfish).

Unfortunately, self-care guilt is a widespread issue. There are five common reasons why you feel guilty about self-care, and I'll explain how to deal with them so you can put your guilt to rest.

And to help you overcome self-care guilt, be sure to download your free copy of the Essential Self-Care Toolkit, which includes three basic tools for beginning to take better care of yourself guilt-free.

Why Do You Feel Guilty About Self-Care?

While it is common to feel guilty about self-care, it is not required. You can let go of the guilt associated with self-care.

The issue is that self-care guilt is complicated – it frequently has multiple causes.

That means that if you want to overcome self-care guilt, you must understand why you feel guilty (or selfish, or as if you need to apologize) whenever you attempt self-care.

Let's dissect the five most prevalent sources of self-care guilt so you can finally prioritize self-care guilt-free.

Reason #1 for Self-Care Guilt: Your Self-Care Definition
When I ask clients experiencing self-care guilt to define self-care, they often struggle to do so. They begin with the most obvious (exercise, getting enough sleep, and eating well).

We can also find that many people define it as a way to feel better, keep in better shape, and get a break from life's many responsibilities. The issue with this definition is that it is both too restrictive and incorrect. And it makes many people feel excessively indulgent (and hence selfish) when they attempt to carve out time for themselves.

How to Reconceptualize Self-Care (the Right Way)
The truth is that self-care is not primarily about feeling good. And it has NOTHING to do with emancipating yourself from your life. [Side note: Being continually on the hunt for an escape route is an indication that you need to take better care of yourself].

Does self-care contribute to your well-being? Naturally (it's a delightful byproduct).

However, many activities that feel good at the moment are not acts of self-care (and can even hurt you in the long term). Additionally, self-care is not synonymous with indulgence. Numerous vices are unhealthy. And viewing it as an indulgence will only add to your guilt, persuading you that it is not necessary (which it is).

Self-care is concerned with the individual's physical, mental, emotional, and spiritual well-being. And that is neither indulgent nor self-indulgent.

Can a visit to the spa be considered self-care? Of course (although doing it weekly may be regarded as an indulgence and goes beyond the call of self-care).

What's important to recognize is that self-care may be far more straightforward than that. Often, the most straightforward self-care routines are the most effective. And you can look after yourself impeccably without ever setting foot in a spa (really). Self-care activities include clearing your thoughts with a 10-minute stroll, reading a book, and contacting your best friend.

Reason #2 for Guilt About Self-Care: Self-Care As A Zero-Sum Game

There is a widespread misconception that prioritizing something entails sacrificing something else. There is a cost associated with this. While this is true for various things, it is not true regarding self-care.

Why Self-Care Isn't Zero-Sum

If you opt to go to the gym over a work happy hour, you have selected one activity above the other. As a result, you may believe that zero-sum logic applies here. However, is this true?

Self-care:
- provides you with the energy to work late when necessary.
- enables you to maintain your composure under duress,

- improves your capacity to concentrate (and so your ability to be most effective at work and home), and
- assists you in maintaining control of your emotions.

You'll be better able to deal with that significant job problem (which has been irritating you for the last week since you're too exhausted to think creatively). Additionally, you'll be less likely to snap at your children and spouse each evening due to stress.

Appropriate self-care empowers you to serve, accomplish, and give more to others (both personally and professionally).

How to Alter Your Equation of Self-Care by Crossing It Off Your To-Do List

The issue is that most individuals view self-care as yet another task to add to their (already lengthy) to-do list. It appears to be a chore.

The equation you are currently utilizing is as follows (in order of priority):

WORK + FAMILY + CHORES + OTHER (including self-care)

Because self-care comes last, it is rarely utilized. And it's the FIRST thing you push aside when you're pressed for time.

The truth is that self-care must occur before this equation is applied. Everything else, even your to-do list, should take a back seat.

Furthermore, self-care is not so much about doing things. It's primarily an attitude issue... a way of life and being.

I know that even contemplating putting yourself first can precipitate an anxiety episode. After all, we've been taught that putting ourselves first is selfish (particularly if you're a parent).

Ask yourself how well you can care for others if you can't care for yourself first. Selfishness is exemplified by those who are dependent on others.

Thus, by neglecting self-care, you are being selfish! How about it for a truly monumental "aha" moment?

Reason #3 for Self-Care Guilt: Success Is Described As Accomplishment

According to most individuals, success is defined as a list of achievements. It's primarily about accomplishing your objectives and meeting specific metrics.

And this is a dilemma since...

Working hard doesn't guarantee success (Or The Quality Of Your Plan)

Life is not fair, and numerous factors outside your control might affect your success. Although your contribution affects the outcome, it is only a small part of the equation.

In what way is self-care guilt involved in any of this?

When you define success as mostly based on achievement (and thus on your input), you are primarily focused on the factors you cannot control, which results in frustration, increased effort, and increased output, to the point that you're likely to feel as though you should be doing something more constructive than relaxing.

You Have Complete Control Over Yourself

While most people think that life is unjust, it's difficult not to push back and act as if life should be just.

The issue is that life is not and never will be fair. Society is made up of flawed, judgmental, and prejudiced individuals, which means true justice will never occur.

Notwithstanding how hard you work or the amount you want, you won't continuously get it. Others may strive harder or simply get lucky. At times, individuals will actively work against you.

Success should not be measured in terms of output but rather of input (i.e., everything from your conduct to your productivity to your self-care and interpersonal interactions).

Keep in mind that attempting to be more fair (or bettering the lives of others) isn't the best strategy; it's just not the best approach to focus solely on fairness. Concentrating on input produces greater results and enables you to redefine success to allow you to be happy while working toward something better (even though the outcome may not be guaranteed, or you might fail). It's possible to include self-care in this new definition of success (you'll be able to provide more valuable input if you take good care of your health).

How You View Success Has an Effect on Your Self-Concept (and Hence Your Self-Worth)

If you define success in terms of accomplishments, your outcome will also predominantly determine your self-worth. Additionally, you are less likely to believe that you are deserving of self-care.

The deal is as follows:

If you value yourself, you will look after yourself. Taking care of yourself has a beneficial ripple effect. It increases your sense of self-worth, self-esteem, and self-confidence.

Additionally, it assists you in being more mentally present, which is a significant difficulty for many high achievers and affects how you feel about yourself. Neglecting your health will result in decreased productivity.

This indicates that good self-care results in increased self-esteem and a more optimistic attitude on life.

Achievement-Based Success Complicates Things

Self-care becomes very difficult when you are achievement-driven since you become fixated on measurements. And this results in you monitoring every calorie you consume, stressing over the number of steps you take each day, and weighing yourself each morning.

Not only is it excessive, but this method gives the sensation of a duty that you despise yet must complete.

Wouldn't you rather think of self-care as something you include naturally throughout your day for your well-being?

Reason #4 for Guilt About Self-Care: You Feel Compelled to Say Yes (To Everyone Except Yourself)

A large number of my clients are worried about this. They feel bound to say yes – even more so if they are being asked to employ a skill or talent they are particularly adept at. And this is especially true when individuals apply it liberally.

The issue is you do not have to commit to something simply because you believe you could do it well (or even better than someone else). Occasionally, the best thing you can do for someone is to say no and let them figure it out for themselves.

The Time Has Come To Say No

I am aware that boundaries may make even the most confident us nervous. It's simple to define where you want them to go but more difficult to execute because it requires saying no.

Saying no isn't about the word "no," as some may believe. Boundaries are used to protect your priorities and preserve your well-being. And there is nothing erroneous about that (or bad about the no for those reasons).

By establishing and enforcing firm boundaries, you demonstrate your respect for yourself.

Saying no to someone means saying yes to yourself and the ones you cherish most at the same time so that you might be the finest version of yourself and serve others to the utmost extent possible.

Reason #5 for Guilt About Self-Care: Your Time Isn't Your Own

Your time is valuable. You own it (no one else does – and I mean no one else).

Stop wasting your time as if it were infinite for the simple reason it isn't. Once spent, you will never receive it back.

Take Control of Your Time by Maintaining a Time Log

When clients tell me they have no time, I require them to keep a weekly diary. Everything they do and how long it takes are recorded (the time spent on social media, checking email while dining, and getting up from their desk for coffee are all examples).

Although they despise this practice (it's tedious), they're constantly surprised at how much time they squander, how much time they spend with loved ones (that they underestimated), and what they say yes to that they shouldn't.

This straightforward practice enables people to alter their perspective on time, how they spend their time, and what they say yes to.

I want you to follow suit. For an entire week, keep track of everything you do and how much time you spend doing it. Maintain a running log. Reflect on how you spent your time (warning: it will shock you) at the end of the week.

Many people spend their time on activities that are well recognized as time-wasters, such as browsing through social media. While these are critical time-wasters to eliminate, there are others (less evident), such as coworker interruptions and time spent reading irrelevant emails.

Utilize your time carefully, safeguard it, and treat it with the reverence it deserves.

The Following Steps Towards Guilt-Free Self-Care
Self-care has been hijacked by a slew of #selfcare social media soothsayers obsessed with sugary sweet slogans and memes but offer no direction on HOW to care for yourself without feeling guilty.

To overcome self-care guilt, three things are required:
- A succinct description of self-care.
- Understanding HOW to begin prioritizing it.
- An effective support system (you can go to for help, guidance, and accountability).

We've already discussed a portion of item #1 (and a portion of item #2). To assist with the remainder, remember to obtain your complimentary copy of the Essential Self-Care Toolkit here:

It is critical to begin simply. Keep in mind that self-care does not have to be difficult. The following is a brief explanation of how to get started:

Self-Care Without Feeling Guilty Step 1: Determine What You Need

It's difficult to know where to direct your attention if you're uncertain about your current location. Simply said, you are stronger in certain areas than others.

Perhaps you enjoy exercising, yet your mind is frequently racing (rarely focused). You are doing well in terms of physical self-care, but not so well in terms of mental self-care.

To prioritize your efforts, you must first decide where you fall on the self-care spectrum for several aspects of self-care. Additionally, please remember that this is not a one-time event. What you require varies daily, depending on your circumstances and the events around you (even within the world). It's critical to check in with yourself frequently to reassess what you truly require.

Step #2 of Guilt-Free Self-Care: Determine What Works (and What Doesn't)

It's astounding how many people perform tasks for self-care that they dislike (because they believe they're required to). If you dislike running, then avoid it. Alternatively, if you're like me and quickly bored, incorporate various exercises such as strength training, walking, HIIT training, and yoga.

The trick is to determine what activities constitute self-care for you. This is what I mean by "knowing your self-care style." Experiment with new stuff. Experiment. Consider daily actions that could qualify as self-care (that you may not be considering) and strategies to include self-care into your regular activities simply.

For instance, I've discovered that my boys are more receptive to the conversation (about real topics) in the car. As a result, I transport them to and from school and baseball as frequently as feasible. This may not qualify as self-care for you, but it is for me. It maintains my mental and spiritual well-being.

Self-Care Without Guilt Step #3: Establish Simple, Flexible Routines and Habits

It's time to use the knowledge learned in stages #1 and #2. Begin by developing a few easy habits that will assist you where you are most in need. I recommend beginning with the following:

- a morning ritual that can help you stay focused and energetic throughout the day; and
- an evening ritual that aids in relaxation and preparation for sleep.

Maintain basic and adaptable routines. For instance, suppose your morning regimen includes exercise and meditation. How much time you spend on those two activities varies each day. On days when you have a lot of time and energy, you might do ten minutes of stretching and an hour of weight training. And your meditation may last between three and fifteen minutes.

Once you've developed a sense of familiarity, expand your routines by developing more habits at work and home. Additionally, ensure that you address all facets of self-care (mental, physical, and spiritual). Consider unconventional solutions!

Bear in mind that conversing with my guys in the van is a form of self-care for me.

This is a way of life (not necessarily about adding a bunch of stuff to your day). To assist you, the following are a few activities I do as part of my self-care regimen (that you may not consider self-care):

- Running or walking with my guys (they normally ride their bikes while I run and walk);
- Playing soccer with my sons outside;
- Being a part of a weekly game night (this keeps you intellectually healthy, is enjoyable, and provides time for you and your loved ones to converse and enjoy one another); and
- Cooking nutritious meals together as a family.

Step #4: Establish a Support System for Guilt-Free Self-Care
You'll require a combination of people and resources (such as a calendar system and apps) to assist you in staying on track and productive. Consider who you trust to be lovingly candid with you (and who you will listen to) when it comes to others. DO NOT INCLUDE ANYONE WHO CAUSES YOU TO EXPERIENCE AN EMOTION OR WHO IS INTERESTED IN YOUR OUTCOME.

Additionally, examine how you might incorporate a natural support system into your regular self-care routines and behaviors. For instance, my youngest son like riding his bike alongside me as I walk/run. Once we began, I promised that we would continue (and established some guidelines for when we would do so regularly). Naturally, he notifies me when it is time for our walk.

Avoid overthinking the assistance you require, but also avoid ignoring this step.

Taking care of yourself doesn't have to be difficult or time-consuming. In addition, it should not arouse feelings of shame or selfishness in the recipient.

Utilize the knowledge above to rethink and reframe self-care so that you may stop feeling guilty for self-care and instead prioritize YOU.

CONCLUSION

There is a huge distinction between "honest mistakes" made by humans and those made by dishonest, manipulative, and even deceitful humans. Children typically learn the not-so-subtle distinction between making mistakes or screwing up and manipulatively concealing them with half-truths, omissions, and falsehoods. When someone acts deceptively, deviously, or deceitfully, the interpersonal trust invested in that person and connection is breached and damaged, sometimes irreversibly and sometimes not.

It's one thing to make mistakes, which human beings do daily if you haven't noticed. That is one thing; lying about it is quite another! When you lie, I simply cannot trust you. Otherwise, all bets are off; I am fooled, partly due to my misguided trust, silly naiveté, and gullibility. Let us say that it does not sit well. There is no way to clear this up as long as the setting is dishonest and manipulatively lying to go somewhere or whatever. I have no choice except to stay away from you until you become trustworthy. As with bad credit, establishing good credit over time will help the bad credit fade away as you rebuild your credit. The remainder of this essay discusses "honest mistakes" made by people and rectifies them.

What can a person do in a world drowning in hurt, errors, snafus, and screw-ups? The time-honored and well-trodden road is to assign blame and fault to someone else. This will absolve you of responsibility, and as a bonus, you will get to skewer and gore someone else's ox. What joy! Typically, the first domino to fall is guilt and shame, followed by retribution for the perpetrator and their awful crimes. Following that, repeat this cycle indefinitely. This is a madman's plan, with our egos or minds assuming the role of a fictional self or an illusory notion of who we believe we are. Its presence on this planet has a lengthy and sad history.

It is a truly enlightening moment when you understand that none of the subsequent dominoes will fall unless the first one does. Similarly, the keystone of a bridge is crucial for the structure's integrity, and the first domino in a line of falling dominoes holds the power of all the other dominoes. It stands with it; without it, it falls. Change how you retain and perceive mishaps cognitively, whether you name them hurt, mistakes, snafus, or screw-ups, and that initial domino is irreversibly modified. Simply change the focus of blunders from fault and blame to accountability, more precisely on owning your part of the responsibility, and the entire pattern pivots nicely.

When you accept your genuine share of responsibility, whether it is 1% or 100% when things go wrong, there is no need for guilt or humiliation and even less reason to beat someone up! Responsibility translates as "response-ability," or the capacity to respond or select. The lovely possibility is to bring the capacity for response and choice into life, both when things go well and when they don't. You could even call this acting like an adult. Adult behavior can occur at any age. And it is astoundingly amazing to discover at any age.

Consider guilt to be feeling awful about something you did that was wrong or hurtful, or, more precisely, the sensation of disgust associated with negative thinking. Thus, existential shame is a fictitious sensation or emotion. Shame is the belief that you are a lousy, awful, or nasty person, accompanied by a sense of disgust and a negative mental assessment.

Existential guilt responds to actual harm, such as physical, cognitive, emotional, or interpersonal injury. Effectively resolving and making peace with guilt is critical for healthy development. Here are two critical elements that serve as a straightforward litmus test for existential guilt: (1) establish that the activity is wrong, such as murder, and (2) establish the real harm committed, such as an injury or violation. In my view, not much qualifies as ethically wrong, even in the extreme case of murder, and not much qualifies as actual harm that is typically committed. If you are aware of either, it is existential guilt; it is not a question of intention. However, the sting is lessened without bringing any intention of harm. Generally, whatever occurred does not constitute existential guilt. Rather than that, it is 'imagined guilt,' in which you believe you have done something wrong but have not. You never looked to verify. Pausing to check for oneself is critical in avoiding carrying something that is not yours.

For most people, one estimate is that of all the guilt they carry and continue to accumulate, possibly 10% at the most and less than 1% at the very least counts as guilt for wrongdoing or direct injury. The remainder is imagined guilt, which is worth acknowledging, releasing, and regaining a sense of self-worth.

In such situations, you can take pleasure in boldly saying, "Cancel and erase," numerous times and instantly replace it with a self-validating phrase, such as "I know I did no harm, I'm a good person, and I can make a difference." In such situations, every one of us can realistically breathe a sigh of relief.

What are your options if, after checking with reality, you or someone else is found to have committed an act of wrongdoing and causing harm, for which you now suffer existential guilt? A basic way to dissolve and make peace with guilt, so completing the experience, can be extremely beneficial for reestablishing healthy relations with yourself and others. This assists in the healing of wounds to an individual's integrity, trustworthiness, honesty, and relationships. Here are five necessary stages, along with two optional steps, to accomplish this completely:

1. Recognition: To begin, awaken, become aware, and observe your behaviors when hurt or errors occur. Determine whether your behaviors, including your words, attitude, and body language, contribute to the subsequent challenges. Consider the following: "Is this conduct of mine illegal, such as murder?" and "Did my activities directly or indirectly result in some hurt, injury, or a violation occurring to another?" If you answered affirmatively to either question, you have acknowledged the harm you contributed to. This is the critical step of recognition or consciousness. Without this critical step, nothing else will occur. "I perceive/see/ acknowledge this injury," you can say.

2. Accountability: Declare publicly your responsibility for any harm that occurred due to or was impacted by your actions. Do express your accountability and ownership directly to

the wounded person or persons; state, "I did this; I own this; I am accountable for this." This is an excellent place to linger, look the other person in the eye, and slowly, truly, and again state what you did and accept responsibility for it.

3. Commitment: Make a two-sided commitment and your word of honor to refrain from repeating this harmful act and to commit to performing only good, responsible actions going forward; state, "I swear to you that this will never happen again, and I'll only do these wonderful, responsible things from now on." Typically, this important phase is skipped. Individuals who receive such a strong two-sided commitment are frequently overjoyed.

4. Repair: Ask what you need to do to repair the harm and put things right again; for example, "I want to make this right with you; what can I do now to put this behind us completely?" Often, merely declaring your possessions suffices. To end the destructive event and put you both behind bars, the loss of property may be demanded. Occasionally, it may be appropriate to somehow help the wounded individual or community. After everything has been expressed honestly, the person who committed the injury can inquire whether the affected person is pleased. This is frequently the case.

5. Release: With the repair completed in the viewpoint of the harmed party, this episode is now concluded; inquire, "Is this now concluded for you?" If this is the case, fantastic! We can both quickly let go of this." Unfortunately, some people are good at harboring grudges and will never let go

of the occurrence. Thankfully, this is a rather infrequent occurrence in my experience. When this occurs, it is appropriate to inform the grudge holder that the incident is over for you; say, "Well, it is over for me, and you may continue to hang onto it if you like." Notably, as long as the detrimental behavior, including addictive behaviors, is not reenacted, it is 'off limits' to bring up during an argument. The conclusion and closure of this occurrence virtually eliminate the possibility of discussing the behavior in the discussion unless the detrimental activities are repeated. When someone has kept their word in action, and the other party wants to bring up an old problem that has not been played out in a long time, this is referred to as "playing low ball" and reflects poorly on the perpetrator. Indeed, it is now up to them to rectify this oversight! However, if the dangerous party resumes the damaging behavior, it is reasonable and acceptable to consider it in the context of a prior history of committing these acts.

Certain individuals with a religious or moral background may wish for those who caused harm to express their regret. If you can say this honestly, that is ok. You may find it more appropriate to state that you felt bad about what you did, a more positive tone shift. The aggrieved party may believe that an apology and a request for forgiveness are also necessary. Consider performing one or both of the following steps as appropriate for the wounded individual in any scenario. It costs you almost nothing; all that is required is your honesty and a desire to put this occurrence fully behind you. It's a little price to pay for such an amazing result. Indeed, it is an excellent deal for everyone.

1. You can express your sorrow for what you did and the hurt you caused by saying, "I feel terrible / I don't feel good about what I did." Now that I'm aware of the consequences, I regret doing it."

2. Apologize verbally and seek forgiveness for what you said or did. Make a point of being explicit about the subject at hand. "I apologize and beg your pardon for saying/doing..."

According to certain authorities, it is preferable to die telling the truth than never confess guilt to prevent causing harm to others. Occasionally, as with past affairs, nothing positive may come from speaking up today, even more so if the conduct has halted long ago and you have honestly changed and matured. You must weigh the potential harm to the injured party that may result from your admission today, as well as the steps are taken to clean it up, against the potential harm that may result from not acknowledging, owning, and cleaning up the incident because it occurred so long ago and under different circumstances, as well as how far you have grown and not repeated the harmful action since then. Constant vigilance and care are necessary to prevent rationalizing wrongdoing to feel more comfortable, avoid potential conflict, and fail to live up to your commitments.

The most difficult choices are not between right and wrong; rather, the most difficult, most difficult, most perplexing options are between two rights. You can make the greatest possible decisions by utilizing insightful reflection, cautious discernment, and the guidance of reputable mentors/consultants, including the indwelling divine. While it is unavoidable that you will make mistakes in this life, it is extremely beneficial to have access to powerful, effective tools that enable you to work through these slip-ups and remove guilt permanently, time after again, until nothing remains. By committing to doing this over and over again, you can fully reclaim the natural serenity, everyday contentment, and majesty of the present moment and dwell and abide in guiltless calm.

Thank you for listening to my thoughts.

If you enjoyed this title and would like to read about other topics that have changed my life, please check out my new books on Amazon or my website: www.my-mindguide.com.

Also, let's stay connected on social media. Please drop a line on Facebook or Instagram, and stay tuned for updates! You're welcome to share your thoughts with me directly as well: gassner@my-mindguide.com. In return, I'll send you a gorgeous infographic that you can cut out and frame.

Also, please leave a review on Amazon, as this will help me to reach an even broader audience. Thank you so much for your time, insight, and undying hunger for knowledge!

I want to say thank you to all of my colleagues, clients, friends, and family members, who have all contributed to what I am now.

I also want to say thank you to Gabriel Palacios, the king of hypnotherapy and a Swiss bestseller author who taught this old fox new tricks, letting me deep-dive into the mystery of hypnotherapy. I learned so much along the journey that I'm now a certified master-hypnosis coach and conversation coach myself!

Furthermore, I want to say thank you to the fantastic teachers of SAMYANA/Bali who trained me to become a certified yoga and meditation teacher.

Last but not least, I give a special thanks to my master-teacher Eckhard Wunderle, who's close to a saint to me. He introduced me to the world of meditation and let me discover all the wonders it has to offer. I couldn't be more proud about having received my certification as a meditation teacher from directly from him at the Institut für Spirituelle Psychologie.

Peace, love, and happiness to all of you—till next time!

CITATIONS

1. Stigler, James W., and Michelle Perry. 1990. "Mathematics Learning in Japanese, Chinese, and American Classrooms." In *Cultural Psychology: Essays on Comparative Human Development*, ed. James W. Stigler, Richard A. Shweder, and Gilbert Herdt. New York: Cambridge University Press.

2. Jump up to:[a] [b] *Woien, Sandra L; Ernst, Heidi A.H; Patock-Peckham, Julie A; Nagoshi, Craig T (2003). "Validation of the TOSCA to measure shame and guilt". Personality and Individual Differences. 35 (2): 313–326. doi:10.1016/S0191-8869(02)00191-5.*

3. [^] *Montes Sánchez, A (2014). "Intersubjectivity and interaction as crucial for understanding the moral role of shame: a critique of TOSCA-based shame research". Frontiers in Psychology. 5: 814. doi:10.3389/fpsyg.2014.00814. PMC 4114200. PMID 25120517.*

[^] *Giner-Sorolla, Roger; Piazza, Jared; Espinosa, Pablo (2011). "What do the TOSCA guilt and shame scales really measure: Affect or action?" (PDF). Personality and Individual Differences. 51 (4): 445–450. doi:10.1016/j.paid.2011.04.010.*

4. Matt, Susan J. 2002. "Children's Envy and the Emergence of the Modern Consumer Ethic, 1890–1930." *Journal of* Social History 36, no. 2: 283–302.

5. Stearns, Peter N. 2003. *Anxious Parents: A History of Modern American Parenting.* New York: New York University Press.

6. Tangney, June Price, and Kurt W. Fischer, eds. 1995. *Self-Conscious Emotions: The Psychology of Shame, Guilt, Embarrassment, and Pride.* New York: Guilford Press.

7. *Harder, David W.; Creenwald, Deborah F. (1999). "Further Validation of the Shame and Guilt Scales of the Harder Personal Feelings Questionnaire-2". Psychological Reports.* **85** *(1): 271–281. doi:10.2466/pr0.1999.85.1.271. PMID 10575992. S2CID 7656273.*

8. Jump up to:[a] [b] *Tangney, June P. (1990). "Assessing individual differences in proneness to shame and guilt: Development of the Self-Conscious Affect and Attribution Inventory". Journal of Personality and Social Psychology.* **59** *(1): 102–11. doi:10.1037/0022-3514.59.1.102. PMID 2213483.*

9. *Robins, R. W., Noftle, E. E., & Tracy, J. L. (2007). Assessing self-conscious emotions: A review of self-report and nonverbal measures. In J. L. Tracy, R. W. Robins, J. P. Tangney, J. L. Tracy, R. W. Robins, J. P. Tangney (Eds.), The self-conscious emotions: Theory and research (pp. 443-467).*

10. Silfver, M., Helkama, K., Lönnqvist, J., & Verkasalo, M. (2008). The relation between value priorities and proneness to guilt, shame, and empathy. Motivation and Emotion Motiv Emot, 69-80.

11. Demos, John. 1988. "Shame and Guilt in Early New England." In *Emotion and Social Change: Toward a New Psychohistory,* ed. Carol Z. Stearns and Peter N. Stearns. New York: Holmes and Meier.

OTHER BOOKS BY THE AUTHOR

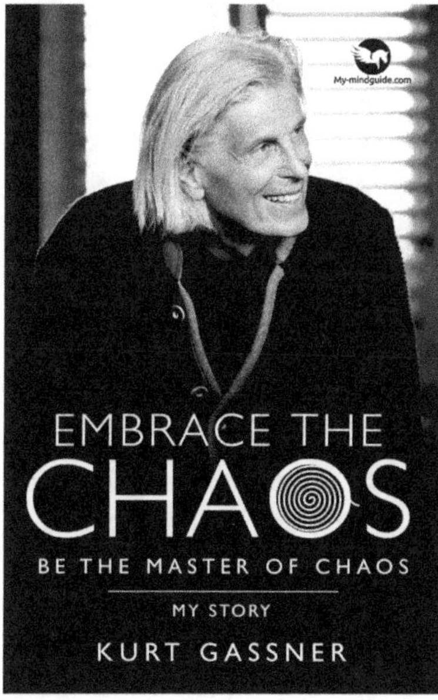

OTHER BOOKS BY THE AUTHOR

OTHER BOOKS BY THE AUTHOR

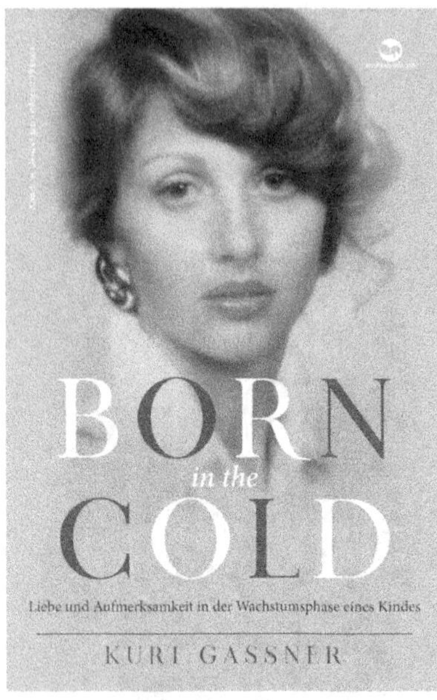
BORN
in the
COLD
Liebe und Aufmerksamkeit in der Wachstumsphase eines Kindes
KURT GASSNER

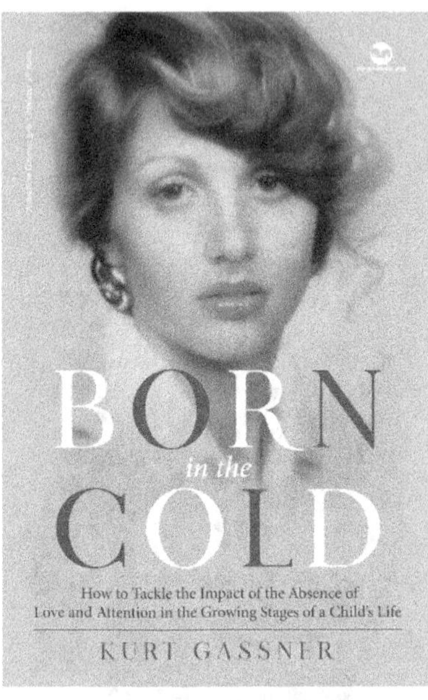
BORN
in the
COLD
How to Tackle the Impact of the Absence of
Love and Attention in the Growing Stages of a Child's Life
KURT GASSNER

SOPHIAS WUNDERWELT
10 ERZÄHLUNGEN
KURT GASSNER

SOPHIA'S WONDERWORLD
10 TALES
KURT GASSNER

BESTSELLING AUTHOR OF
The Art Of
FORGIVNESS
AMAZON #1 BESTSELLER
My-mindguide.com
A practical guide for self healing and overcome past traumas
The Art Of
FORGIVNESS
KURT GASSNER